FIRST DATES

The Art of Love

FRED SIRIEIX

With thanks to Jordan Paramor
and Matt Whyman

VIKING

an imprint of

PENGUIN BOOKS

VIKING

UK | USA | Canada | Ireland | Australia
India | New Zealand | South Africa

Viking is part of the Penguin Random House group of companies
whose addresses can be found at global.penguinrandomhouse.com.

First published 2016
001

Text design by Hampton Associates, Aberdeen
Typeset by Hampton Associates, Aberdeen
Colour reproduction by Rhapsody Ltd, London
Printed in Italy by L.E.G.O S.p.A

A CIP catalogue record for this book is available from the British Library

ISBN: 978–0–241–27987–8

www.greenpenguin.co.uk

MIX
Paper from
responsible sources
FSC
www.fsc.org   FSC® C018179

Penguin Random House is committed to a
sustainable future for our business, our readers
and our planet. This book is made from Forest
Stewardship Council® certified paper.

"

Love is the beauty of the soul.

"

SAINT AUGUSTINE

MENU

MENU

༄ ⌇ FIRST WORDS ⌇ ༄

The *First Dates* restaurant teaches us that everyone cherishes love, and all of us carry a deep desire to be surrounded by love.

Love is both everywhere around us and within us, and it is up to us to feel it and see it. Once we do that, we can truly believe in our hearts that we will find the relationship we've been seeking all our lives.

Growing up in Limoges, France, I always wanted to do something with my life that was different. A friend of mine was a pastry chef; I thought what he was doing seemed exciting, so I went to study it at catering college. I enjoyed myself and I learned so much, but I felt too constricted being hidden away in a kitchen all the time.

As part of the course I learned about the service side of things and that felt like more of a challenge. As a result, I ended up switching my focus to front of house, and when I finished my course aged 20 I moved to London to learn English. I got a job in a three-star Michelin restaurant called La Tante Claire and I never looked back. I later returned to college to do a management and leadership degree, and for twenty-five years I have been working in restaurants in the very best London places.

I was lucky: from a young age my parents gave me unconditional love, and that instilled in me the confidence and self-esteem to do whatever I wanted. Having self-esteem enables you to take on any challenges that come your way. It also gives you the inner strength and faith to get up and fight some more whenever you are down. My parents always told me that to be the best you have to seek out the best, so that is what I've always tried to do. I work with people who challenge me and make me better.

In the service industry you've got to understand and like people. You need a basic knowledge of human nature and psychology: what makes people tick. You can't do any of that unless you understand yourself. I have twenty-five years of knowledge of people from my time in restaurants, and I have learned so much from meeting and observing people. I am always learning, and that's the beauty of life.

I've been fortunate to have had a wonderful career. In 2013 I was awarded Manager of the Year at the Cateys, which are like the Oscars of the restaurant world. When that happened I thought, 'I could retire now.' But of course then I started aiming for other goals.

I am currently general manager at the Michelin-starred restaurant Galvin at Windows, and I have created a hospitality training programme, The Art of Service. I'm also very proud of my charity, The Right Course (therightcourse. org.uk), which creates pop-up restaurants in prisons to teach young offenders new skills and learn the value of hospitality. Ultimately this can help them to get jobs once they leave. The plan is to open a number of restaurants in prisons, which won't use any taxpayers' money. It is a very exciting, worthwhile project.

When I was asked to take the reins at the *First Dates* restaurant I was confident in the show from the start, because I trusted the production team and I loved all the people involved. I only want to do good things I can be proud of and show my children; that was the prerequisite for me taking on the role of maître d'.

It is an amazing show to work on and seems to resonate with people so strongly. In the last year alone over 100,000 people have applied to date at the restaurant, which says it all.

The show feels different to anything we have ever had on TV before, because it is warm and generous. It is true and genuine and not cynical. We have 80-year-olds coming on dates and discussing the war, and then we have young people who are nervous and inexperienced. We love an eclectic mix.

We invite normal, everyday people to dine at the restaurant. The daters feel like they could be your mum or your cousin or your brother, so people watching can relate to them. Everyone is rooting for the daters. I feel like the show and the people who watch it are kind.

First Dates is so popular because it is a joy to experience, for those involved in the date as well as those watching at home. The intentions of the team are pure, with the sole aim being to get like-minded people together and create happiness. There is no sinister agenda behind it. It is genuine and it is true.

The *First Dates* restaurant is located near St Paul's Cathedral in London. Everyone who is dining in there when we film is on a real date. Part of my role in the restaurant is to make people feel calm and welcome when they arrive. I want the date to work as much as the couple do.

As soon as I speak to two people who are going on a date, I can usually tell if it is going to work. I sense the vibes and whether they're going to get along. Then, when their eyes meet, it says it all. I know within a second whether they like each other.

First Dates is about dating and love, but ultimately it is about people. That means it's about all of us – it's almost an anthropological nature programme. *First Dates* never pulls any punches. The truth is always plain for everyone to see, and it's as honest as can be. From watching the episodes it is also reassuring to see that there is no such thing as 'normal'. It teaches all of us about ourselves and life, and reminds us all how unique and special we are.

THE ART OF THE MATCH

We are all looking for love in some shape or form, and the restaurant is all about the dates. It is not about the food or the service – they are an added bonus. What is important is that people get together. And that has to start with the right people meeting each other.

When we are planning the dates at the restaurant, we look to meet about eighty people a week, who we have carefully selected from the hundreds of thousands of people who have applied. We have a team dedicated to reading through the applications and speaking to hopeful singletons on the phone, before inviting them to meet us in person to find out what really makes them tick.

> *We take into consideration what they're looking for, and more importantly what they think they want versus what they might need.*

After meeting hopeful daters we create cards for each dater with all the little details and preferences that will help us find their perfect match. These are stuck up on boards and the whole team work together to match people, passionately discussing every individual's preferences, tastes, life experience, hobbies – you name it – in the hope that this common ground or shared experience could be what creates a spark.

We take into consideration what they're looking for, and more importantly what they think they want versus what they might need. Sometimes it is just a feeling we go with.

People's values and dreams have to be similar, too. It doesn't matter if one of you loves sci-fi films and the other one doesn't. Those kinds of things aren't deal breakers. We feel a genuine responsibility to match people well and we do not want to go for stereotypes.

Someone has got to be pretty shallow if they are only looking for a mirror image of themselves.

Reality is the key to clarity. If someone comes along and they are clear about what kind of person they want to meet – and we're not talking a 'perfect' person here – that makes it easier to match them to someone who thinks in the same way they do.

Sometimes there can be very strong similarities between a couple, like Gareth and Suzie who both loved pug dogs. On the surface it seemed like they would get on, and they talked non-stop about pugs to start with, but ultimately the crucial chemistry wasn't there. Then there are Ashley and Sonia, the scientist and the single mum. Some might say they weren't an obvious match. Then they met, and fate took over. At the end of the day we are all individuals so we will never find someone who is exactly the same as us. We are unique and that is to be celebrated.

> 6 *In the pursuit of love, we learn a great deal about ourselves.* 9

Naturally, everyone wants to know about the success stories. How many singletons found their soulmate here and lived happily ever after? Well, we don't put tracking devices on people after they leave the restaurant, or monitor how long they see each other for. Our role is to help that first spark.

But we do know that many of the couples go straight on to a bar or club, and end up having a fun night together. As for the longer term, while it is lovely that some couples go on to tie the knot, like Scott and Victoria, or Adam and Dan, what matters for me is that everyone who faces a stranger across a candlelit table leaves with an invaluable experience.

In the pursuit of love, we learn a great deal about ourselves, and that can only serve us well in life. It is fascinating to watch this process unfurl before our eyes, from little things like a fleeting glance to an awkward pause, or personal revelations that can change the dynamic in a heartbeat. There is drama here as much as romance, comedy and even tragedy. In essence, *First Dates* provides a stage and a spotlight. Whether or not love strikes before the curtain closes, we are enlightened by every story that plays out.

THE *FIRST DATES* ALTERNATIVE

Before the Internet we used to meet our potential partners at work or in a bar, but these days life is fast-paced and technology means we are constantly connecting with each other through social media and apps. We can meet people in so many other ways, but some of them feel like they have no depth.

We find a lot of people who apply for a date in the restaurant have reached the end of their tether when it comes to online dating and the disposability of it. They come to us because they want to meet someone and are intrigued as to who we might match them with – because it could just be the right person for them.

The problem with apps is that you always think you can do better. It does not cost you money, it is easy access and you can confuse a meaningful relationship with quick, casual sex, which probably is not the thing you're looking for (but of course if you are, that is fine, too).

Ultimately love will always remain the same, but a date in the restaurant provides the antidote to dating through apps or social media. It is a back-to-basics, blind introduction of two like-minded people over dinner. There are no preconceptions or trickery involved, and no opportunity to Google-stalk beforehand. It is just a good old-fashioned meeting of minds over a delicious meal.

❝ It is a back-to-basics, blind introduction of two like-minded people over dinner. ❞

SECRET HEROES

The reason the staff at the restaurant work together so well is because they are fundamentally nice people and they make it a fun place to be. We are all respectful of each other, and we like each other. We all know how lucky we are and we work as a team – you need to do that to make it special. At the end of the night we stay on after the guests have left and we have a drink and chat about how everything has gone.

Merlin is like a walking encyclopedia; he is interested in the origins of everything. His bar area is a bit of a sanctuary before the daters sit down to dinner. He asks very practical questions and makes people feel at ease.

CiCi and Laura both have this amazing quality: men and women love them because they are so open and welcoming. CiCi has a more whimsical outlook on love and life and wants to be swept away by a prince. Laura is a bit more girl-next-door and sporty, and more pragmatic when it comes to love.

Sam represents many men in the world and he's so funny. We always say he is like a big, joyous Labrador. CiCi is always trying to teach Sam how to act with women, and their conversations are pure comedy.

MAGIC MOMENTS

There have been so many classic moments on First Dates, but these are among my highlights so far.

» **FRANKIE AND MUHALA**
They were so much fun; Frankie's laugh brought me joy.

» **JO AND NAOMI**
I knew straight away it was going to work. I love that they are still together.

» **ROSIE AND PAUL**
They bonded over Metallica, but after the date they decided not to see each other again. Then they both watched the show, arranged to meet up again and they have been together ever since.

» **ADAM AND DAN**
They make perfect sense together and I was overjoyed when they got engaged. They love each other so much.

» **SCOTT AND VICTORIA**
They are as quirky as each other and they are so happy. They fit together so well and I am so excited that they're getting married.

It is incredible to think that some people will spend the rest of their lives together as a result of being on *First Dates*. The pay-off from working on the show is pretty rewarding. Sometimes people come along to the restaurant expecting just to have a bit of fun – they do not expect to meet the love of their life, but it happens.

We keep up to date with people once the show ends and like to hear how they are doing. It makes us happy when we discover that people have fallen in love and everything is working out well for them.

CELEBRITIES NEED LOVE, TOO

The one-off shows, such as the celebrity specials, have been intense. It is fascinating to see how people react when they are set up with a well-known face. It is interesting to see if they just see a famous individual, or if they look deeper to find the person behind the public image.

When you are in the public eye people think they already know you, but you may be a totally different person to who you are on TV. Celebrities get lonely, too; they get sad when they're watching Netflix on their own on a Sunday night. So if we can help them to find someone fabulous, then why not?

We've had some great people on the celebrity specials. The first episode with Jorgie Porter, Jamie Laing, Anthea Turner and Alexandra Burke was supposed to be a one-off for Stand Up to Cancer, and it was brave of the celebrities to take part. Those dates went so well and people loved the episode so much we ended up doing a whole series, which was every bit as much fun.

Celebrities such as Jess Wright, Richard Blackwood, Scarlett Moffatt from Gogglebox, Esther Ranzen and Brad Simpson from The Vamps came along to try and find love, and once again it was fascinating to see how people reacted when they arrived at the restaurant to find their date was someone famous. There were some very funny and very touching moments.

THAT SPECIAL SPARK

I hope you enjoy what we have in store for you here, and that it proves to be both entertaining and illuminating on different levels. Personally, it has been a wonderful adventure for me to explore the nature of love and reflect on so many incredible First Dates moments.

My intention in this book is to guide you through every stage of the dating process, from the nervous expectation to that giddy introduction, the bonding moments and the thrill that comes with recognizing there is a spark that could lead to something special. Love at first sight is a precious thing, but it doesn't strike every couple, so how can you tell if it's worth kindling or if there's a friendship here that could endure? Then we have the question of how to handle a date that doesn't go to plan, and how you can look back on the evening without wishing to change a single thing. There is a great deal to consider here, and together with my team we trust that *First Dates: The Art of Love* will find a place in your heart.

Having introduced each chapter with my thoughts and reflections, I invite our most memorable daters to look back upon their time in the restaurant and shed light on the experience. I also have CiCi, Laura and Sam on hand to offer their perspective, insight and advice. They have a great deal to offer, having served so many tables in such fine fashion. Along the way you'll also find my Finest Moments from the show. As well as highlights that had everyone talking, you'll also find observations that reveal so much about our search for love and, ultimately, the human condition. With this in mind, may the pages that follow provide entertainment, insight, reassurance and advice about that life-affirming quality that can spring from a simple first date.

Hopes & Dreams

Chapter One

ON KNOWING YOURSELF

We all start dreaming of love when we are children, and as we get into our teens we have an idea of what we want that love to be like when it appears. We watch Disney movies, and films like *Pretty Woman*, and create our own films inside our head. They are always filled with fantasy and they are usually wildly unrealistic, but we have a fun time directing them.

We dream about this amazing relationship and how it will play out, and we imagine how our life will be with that special person. We see the union from start to end; from the first date and meeting the parents to getting married and having children. It all feels like a fairy tale with you starring as the prince or princess. But once you are actually in a relationship, things change. You have to live with each other's down points and work at things, because the reality is that love is not textbook. None of us are perfect, so we should not seek out perfection in other people either.

You have to be careful that your dreams aren't unobtainable. You have to know what you want, but you also have to know that you may need to compromise on certain things because no one is going to have every quality you yearn for. In short, there is no such thing as the 'perfect' partner, but you can still make your relationship an incredibly happy one.

As Shakespeare said, expectation is the root of all heartache, and if you have false expectations and desires, they are going to get in the way of meeting someone who is right for you. It is about digging deep and finding that truth within, not focusing on an illusion. You have to really know what you want and not what other people or the media may tell you. You need to be brave and believe in your own truth. If you cannot be true to yourself, you can never meet the one who is right for you.

Two people's ideas of love can be completely different but they may have a connection, and that is what is important, because that is what you can build on. As long as you have common ground you have a lot. Sometimes you just have to give someone a chance. But equally, it is important to admit when someone is not right for you. If you know that 'special something' is not there after several dates, it is not going to magically appear – no matter how much you want it to.

Don't try to rush love or hold on to something that is not real. Some people treat dating as if it is a race to the finish line, but it is not. It is the hardest marathon you'll ever run and it may take blood, sweat and tears. But at the end of it you could come away with an incredible medal, and that will be worth waiting for.

Keep an open mind when it comes to what you desire, but be very honest with yourself and approach the world of dating with your eyes wide open. Love is such a wonderful thing when it is real.

> **Don't try to rush love or hold on to something that is not real.**

HOW WAS IT FOR YOU?

SCOTT

VICTORIA

'Part of me thought that if I met an amazing person then I'd be ready.'

People come to the *First Dates* restaurant from all walks of life, but everyone arrives hoping they'll have a good time. Whether you're up for a laugh or something more serious, it's natural to want to find someone you connect with on different levels. For Scott and Victoria, their experience didn't just result in a second date, but one heartfelt romance and a marriage proposal.

The couple are now house-hunting in South London ahead of their wedding, but was this fairy-tale ending something either of them expected when they first walked through the door? 'No way,' they chime, before Scott explains that he was simply looking for a new experience. 'A year beforehand, I'd broken up with a long-term girlfriend. After that, I had twelve months of fun, but the fact is I turn 40 this year. So, while I would've been happy to have just had a laugh, I was also open to something more serious with the right person.' Victoria had also reached a point in life when she wanted something deeper than her previous relationships offered. 'I just didn't want to waste their time or mine,' she explains. 'All I could think was that if I'm with someone but we're not going to settle down and have kids then we might as well shake hands and move on. I genuinely went into the restaurant hoping to have a good time, but a part of me thought that if I met an amazing person then I'd be ready.'

Even with Fred on hand to welcome guests and put them at ease, both Scott and Victoria were deeply nervous before meeting. 'I was first in,' says Victoria. 'Whenever a guy came through the door, I just assumed it was my date. None of them looked right for me, of course, and that just made me feel even more tense. Then Scott arrived, and I have to say that I was impressed. He was smiley, which is a big plus for me. The only thing is I had him down as being much younger than he actually is,' she admits. 'I felt that only someone older could bring out the best in me, so it was a relief to learn that I was a few years out.' As for Scott, his strategy to play it cool fell by the wayside as soon as he laid eyes on his date. 'Victoria had me on my toes from the start,' he says. 'She's a bit of a joker, which was great, but any attempt to play it cool just got lost in an evening that felt like it was moving at a hundred miles an hour.'

While it was clear to the nation that Scott and Victoria shared a spark that would take them beyond a first blind date, did either of them anticipate feeling such a strong attraction? 'It just happened as we learned more about each other,' explains Scott. 'We had so much in common that even our individual quirks seemed to complement each other. Victoria has her thing about numbers, and in the same way I'm always switching off lights whenever I leave a room. They're both unusual forms of behaviour, if you like, but we're coming from the same place and it works.' Victoria agrees. 'We're the tidiest couple we know,' she adds, as Scott chuckles wryly. 'Everything is so ordered.'

For many people, even a first date that turns out better than expected might not lead to something deeper. When did Scott and Victoria realize that they had found soulmates in each other? 'We met up again the very next day,' says Scott. 'Victoria's mum invited us for supper. As soon as I arrived, it was clear that we were both still buzzing, and that just carried on as we talked.' Victoria shared the same feeling. Despite having only just met, she even offered Scott her car so he could drive home. 'I live in London and he's based down near the coast,' she says. 'I just offered him the key because it felt like a natural thing to do. I trusted him then as I do now, but it was still quite chilled between us.' According to Scott it took a few weeks for things to develop. 'Eventually, we just wanted to be with each other all the time,' he says, 'and now look where we are.'

> 6 *We're talking about strangers coming together, sharing their stories and then seeing where it takes them on limited time.* 9

'We feel so blessed,' says Victoria, reflecting on just how far they've travelled. 'What are the chances of a blind date working out so well?' Scott agrees, and looks on his time in the restaurant as life-changing. 'We could've parted company and never seen each other again,' he says. 'We're talking about strangers coming together, sharing their stories and then seeing where it takes them on limited time. It's a one-chance sort of deal, and you have to make the most of it. I can safely say I've never talked as much on a date as I did when I met Victoria.'

As one of the poster couples for a blind date that worked out in every conceivable way – including a Haribo ring proposal at the bar on their Christmas return – what advice do Scott and Victoria have for anyone else hoping to find love through a first date? 'Just be yourself,' says Victoria. 'It's natural to hope that you're going to meet someone nice, but if you're unrealistic then chances are you'll be disappointed. It would also be very easy to dismiss someone straight away because they don't match such expectations. The fact is you need time to get to know each other. By keeping an open mind then you can only be pleasantly surprised if things work out.' It's a view Scott shares, and voices with one simple conclusion. 'I went in because I thought it would be good dating experience,' he says. 'I came out with a wife.'

SAM SAYS

Scott and Victoria were supposed to meet each other in that place and at that time. I served them and could tell there was something between them from the first moment.

Scott was in the right position to find a very beautiful lady to settle down with, and Victoria fitted the bill perfectly. It was the same for her; Scott was exactly what she was looking for. It was like they were both in the same position at the same time and it just worked. There was no messing about and they both laid their cards on the table. It just clicked.

They seemed to enjoy every second of their date and I respect them for taking a leap when they'd both experienced break-ups. That's what love is about – taking a risk and getting back up and trying again if you get hurt. I love the fact they're engaged. It is a huge joy when two people find each other in the *First Dates* restaurant. I bet Scott and Victoria gave hope to a lot of people watching.

My advice to anyone who wants to find love would be to be brave. I've found love, lost it, and found it again several times over the years. I've thought someone was right and then they weren't and things went wrong, and of course heartbreak is disheartening. But if you don't try again you could be missing out on something so special.

When it comes to love throw yourself into situations and give everything a go, but be responsible and don't do anything that will hurt anyone else. Don't lead anyone on, because that's the worst thing you can do. Honesty is important, as is being yourself. If you pretend to be someone totally different and put on a front you may as well have sent someone else on that date instead of you.

> ❛ *I've found love, lost it, and found it again.* ❜

If you're worried about being hurt, remember Scott and Victoria. It's always better to wonder why you did something than why you didn't, because at least then you know.

UP CLOSE & PERSONAL

READ MY LIPS
JOHN & SARAH

Sarah is deaf, and an accomplished lip reader. Even so, she explains, some people are just hard to interpret. As a result, past 'communication breakdowns' have made managing relationships a challenge. So when Sarah arrives at the restaurant, she just hopes her date will be someone she can understand. She's nervous when John, 47, rocks up, but the relief on her face is evident when he introduces himself and she reads him like a book. For her date is courteous, kind, intelligent – and, 'He makes me laugh,' she discovers. As for John, when they head off for post-date drinks, he thanks Fred for his hospitality and says simply, 'She's amazing.'

PICTURE THIS
CARL & ANN-MARIE

This is a big moment for Ann-Marie, and not just because she's on a blind date. She's turning 50 today and having survived four bouts of cancer feels that 'time is precious'. So, when 46-year-old Carl sweeps in, looking dapper and with bags of charm, it looks like this is one birthday she'll treasure for a long time to come. By chance, Carl's even brought her a present: a framed photo of himself. Ann-Marie's face is a picture to match, but she quickly overcomes the moment to enjoy an evening with a new-found friend.

FAMILY FIRST
FADI & CLAIRE

'We hold out high hopes for everyone who comes to us,' Merlin assures Jordanian-born divorcé and devoted dad of two, Fadi, as he waits nervously at the bar. This is Fadi's first date since his separation. When single mum Claire arrives, he discovers she's equally anxious, and they quickly bond over the fact that it can be hard to find the time for romance with children in tow. 'I love it when I get to go out,' she says at one point. 'We deserve it,' Fadi agrees, and proves to be so attentive, genuine and enchanting that he dazzles Claire.

THIS GOLDEN AGE
DAVID & MARGARET

Retired bookmaker David's days at the races may be over, but this thoroughbred isn't putting himself out to pasture just yet. 'I'm a bit of a chancer,' he says, 'and some women find that exciting.' As a betting man, however, he puts the odds of finding romance at his age at '500 to 1' and freely admits not many people would take a punt on that. Then again, he's yet to meet his blind date, retired factory girl Margaret. As the pair share stories of growing up during the Blitz, David begins to realize this is a two-horse race that he really should be backing. The evening ends with kisses, and the promise to see each other again. We're reminded that it's never too late to find love.

⚘ ⚘ **AND FINALLY** ⚘ ⚘

To be happy in life we must all have hopes and we must all have dreams. Hope is what keeps us moving forward and gets us through our hardest times, and dreams are somewhere we can escape to. When hopes and dreams combine they are even stronger and anything can be achieved.

Keep an open mind and an open heart. Never lose sight of what you want, but always be willing to compromise, because someone may not be what you perceive to be 'perfect', but they may be perfect for you – flaws and all.

"

*Every heart
sings a song,
incomplete, until
another heart
whispers back.*

"

PLATO

Ready, Steady, Date

Chapter Two

ON BEING YOURSELF, AND SHINING BRIGHT

Building self-confidence before a date is important. That is true whether you're going back to dating after some time away from it, or if you went on a date two nights ago.

What is self-confidence? It is when you believe in yourself and you have faith and trust in yourself and your abilities. You believe in the goodness of your heart and you know who you are. You have self-esteem and you love yourself. I don't think you can ever truly love someone else until you love yourself. So how do you learn to love yourself? You accept yourself exactly as you are.

There are different kinds of confidence. Some people can be very confident at work, but when you put them into a relationship situation they freeze. Some people are very loud when they're with friends, but if you put them in a room with a crowd of strangers they become shy.

> ❛ *I don't think you can ever truly love someone else until you love yourself.* ❜

The confidence I'm talking about is appreciating and accepting yourself. You need to be able to work with your weaknesses as well as your strengths. That is key.

And how do you 'build' that self-confidence? Building implies that you're starting from the ground up, and so this element has a lot to do with what you tell yourself. Those who embrace every aspect of their lives with passion achieve everything they set out to do. In order to believe something, you must tell yourself you can do it over and over again.

And be careful what you tell yourself. Use only positive affirmations and good things will begin to happen.

When we're teenagers growing up we all have our hang-ups; sometimes we carry them around like a ball and chain. Some people let them go when they become adults, but other people carry them around for the rest of their lives and never give themselves a chance. How can you be free if you are carrying around something so heavy?

The thing that holds us back is our fear that we won't get what we want or we'll be inadequate. But we won't get what we want if we live by fear. Fear only exists in our mind. Until we convince ourselves we can let it go, it will be there.

Personal change and development is the hardest thing. Changing who you are is not easy. You need to be self-aware in order to build self-confidence. You have to look inside and accept and like what you see and remember that no human being is perfect. Our faults can also be our strengths.

God gave us free will and we have choices. Every choice we make has consequences, but if you make choices wisely about who you want to be and how you want to live your life, you can change your life.

HOW WAS IT FOR YOU?

LOUIS

'As I approached the restaurant doors, the feeling that I might not be good enough just amplified in my mind.'

'Chivalry has always been very important to me,' says 25-year-old linguist Louis, who melted the heart of a nation with his attempts to find love not once but twice in the *First Dates* restaurant. 'I want my date to feel appreciated and aware that I'm excited about meeting them. It shows I'm willing to make the effort, I think, which lays down the foundations for a good relationship.' These are wise words from this thoughtful, courteous young man with a tendency for introspection. 'At the same time, I do feel the pressure beforehand to get it right,' he admits, 'and that's where I can overthink things.'

Confidence never used to be an issue for Louis. It was the end of his first serious relationship, several years ago, that caused him to review what he had to offer. 'I can be very self-conscious and question whether I'm saying the right thing,' he admits candidly. 'Often, I can start analysing myself mid-sentence,' he adds. 'As a result, I start to stumble, or lose my train of thought, which can make things more of a challenge for me.'

While being himself didn't come easily to Louis, he come to the *First Dates* restaurant with a genuine desire to meet someone suitable. The next hurdle was getting ready to face a stranger. 'Without any idea of their interests or personality, I began to panic a little,' he says. 'I like to go into these situations with some questions I can fall back on. So, working out what to ask someone I'd never met before wasn't easy, and this just contributed to my fear that I might come across badly. It certainly became something I dwelled upon ahead of my date. As I approached the restaurant doors,' he recalls, 'the feeling that I might not be good enough just amplified in my mind. Physically, my heart was pounding and my stomach tightened up. These are things you might expect but only experience can make things easier. It certainly didn't help my immediate situation.'

That evening Louis met assured brunette Adela, and what confidence he had deserted him. They got on well, but having tripped over his tongue on several occasions it was no surprise to see them leave as friends. Louis is quick to identify what went wrong. 'I got myself preoccupied with being chivalrous,' he says. 'I didn't want to lay it on too thick, but needed to show that I was interested. It was just one more thing to think about, and in the end it got the better of me.'

Louis was disappointed. Even so, he considered himself to be down and not out. Part of this, he explains, is linked to his long-term approach to dating, and his belief that a shaky start can be overcome. 'It's always nice to meet someone and have an instant connection, but it isn't always a necessity,' he explains. 'Sometimes, it takes two dates to work things out.'

While he has every respect for Adela's decision, Louis' return to the restaurant for a second attempt was driven by a short, intense period of reflection. 'I came away feeling like I hadn't projected myself well enough, but having been in once I knew I had to change that. It made me determined to find a more positive headspace. You have to believe you'd make a good partner for someone. For me that meant being less harsh on myself. It was also fortunate that I didn't have long before I got the chance to return. Otherwise, I might've just dwelled on things too much, or even lost sight of the mistakes I'd made. As a linguist, they say you need to act on an experience to truly learn from it,' he says, 'and that was definitely the case for me when I met Lydia.'

In a sense, Louis' date with the 23-year-old nanny from London proved that less preparation could help him to relax. 'I knew what to expect the second time around. Lydia was a stranger, of course, but I realized that I didn't need to have lots of questions planned. It risks making the whole date feel like a job interview, which kills any fun or possible romance. It took a bit of courage to go in without anything lined up. I just told myself that it was just one more thing to remember, and potentially one more stumbling block. Instead,' he explains proudly, 'I went in determined to listen more. I was also very transparent at the start about the fact that I had a tendency to lose my train of thought. Once I'd explained that it was no reflection on her, and just a personality quirk of mine, it allowed me to get beyond the early stage I sometimes find so difficult.'

❝ It's all preparation for the last first date I'll ever have. ❞

It was a delight to watch Louis overcome his anxieties and come into his own on his second date. Unfortunately, in his own words, 'life got in the way' of any romance. 'We've been in touch, but haven't managed to see each other,' he says. 'We live in different cities, which makes it hard to be spontaneous about going out. Even so I learned from the experience, and now I approach dates feeling far less negative about myself. I find putting on a nice shirt and cologne helps me to feel prepared. It doesn't necessarily make me feel more relaxed but it helps me to feel good when I meet someone new. Having lost my natural confidence, it's nice to be able to build up that side of things again.'

Louis also credits the public's warm response to his appearances in the restaurant for his new-found assurance ahead of dates. 'It was a lovely surprise,' he says. 'It made me realize that I do have lots to offer, and that I can be likeable. Yes, I have vulnerabilities, but I no longer allow that to get the better of me. I might not be the sort of assertive person you'll see on *The Apprentice*, but I can be myself now, and enjoy the process of looking for that person who could become a partner for life. Ultimately,' he finishes brightly, 'it's all preparation for the last first date I'll ever have.'

LAURA SAYS

Poor Louis put so much thought into his first date that it got the better of him. He knew his nerves would be an issue. Unfortunately, that just became something he grew to fear. So when, with Adela, he lost his train of thought early on it was inevitable he'd go into a panic. From that moment it was always going to be tough to pull it back.

Do you know what made it so heartbreaking? We all loved Louis. Not just the staff in the restaurant but everyone who watched him try so hard with Adela. Here was someone whose confidence was a bit shaky when it came to dating, but who so badly wanted to create the right impression. Haven't we all been there?

Then Louis began to work out that nerves weren't necessarily a sign of failure, but evidence that he cared. As a result he set aside all the planning he'd done for his date with Adela, and came back to meet Lydia with little more than some self-belief that he could make this work. That must've taken some guts. It's a bit like walking into a presentation and leaving your notes behind. With the right frame of mind, however, it's also the surest way to come across in a winning way.

> **❛ Go in with an open mind, a listening ear and a sense of fun, and everything will turn out just fine. ❜**

From watching Louis' experience, and talking to other First Daters who came back for a second shot, my advice is to go in without any expectation whatsoever. Sometimes you have to learn this from experience, like a trial by fire, but it does seem to work. For a start it cuts right down on the temptation to imagine who you might be meeting. There's no need to draw up a list of questions for them, or consider best- and worst-case scenarios.

Instead, go in with an open mind, a listening ear and a sense of fun, and everything will turn out just fine. Whatever happens you'll have done your best in meeting someone new. It has to beat building things up in your mind and fretting. This date is there to meet you, not the carefully rehearsed version that hides your true nature. It's a question of having faith in the fact that you have lots to offer.

UP CLOSE & PERSONAL

MAN OR MOUSE?
FRANK & NISHA

With his primped hair, bold earring and finest pink blazer, our Frank arrives at the restaurant sartorially assured. On the inside, by his own admission, he's a quivering wreck. Just walking into the *First*

Dates restaurant is one of the biggest challenges he's ever faced. We might not be party to the pep talk he gave himself in front of his wardrobe mirror, but as he waits for his date we're rooting for him. 'Are you nervous?' asks CiCi, who spots Frank's knees trembling and seeks to reassure him. 'A little bit,' he says, in one of the understatements of the series.

OVERCOMING OBSTACLES
BEN & CHARLOTTE

As Fred says, 'Tough times make us who we are today,' and Ben is a case in point. Following an accident that left him with a serious brain injury, Ben has had to go back to basics – not just in life but love. 'I'm getting there,' says this witty 33-year-old from Manchester. 'It's only taken

twelve and a half years.' Then Ben meets fellow Mancunian Charlotte, 26, who's determined to overcome her confidence issues. While it's clearly taken a great deal of courage for the pair to get through the door, the date proves to be the making of them both. 'I was attracted to you,' she offers bravely at the end, which leaves Ben blushing but not quite lost for words. 'She's lovely,' he says. 'She's great, and I'd like to spend more time with her.' The result? A second date in their home city that sees Ben show off his home-cooking skills.

THE GIFT OF FORESIGHT
GARY & NICOLE

While some people might enter into a date and just wing it, others prefer to plot out the opening stages and leave nothing to chance. 'It's important to have ideas about what you're going to talk about,' suggests Gary, and bravely reveals his talent at reading minds. 'Go on,' she says, and prepares to be amazed. Gary sits back, his eyes searching hers. 'So . . . you've got a cat,' he declares, and it's Nicole who blinks first. 'Um, no,' she says, smiling all the same, because frankly she's a dream date that Gary will want to see again. 'I actually really don't like cats.'

END OF THE LINE
ANDREW & SARAH

The dating game doesn't come naturally to 35-year-old computer programmer Andrew, which is why he arrives at the restaurant reliant on a pre-prepared question in case things start to falter. On meeting Sarah it quickly becomes clear that he's dazzled by her presence – and a little tongue-tied. So when the awkward silences become excruciating, Andrew plays his ace card. 'If you could name a new London Underground line,' he asks, 'what would you call it?' To be fair to Sarah, the long pause that follows would be hard for anyone to fill as a gateway into a magical evening. The couple part company as friends, but we're rooting for Andrew to recognize that this is a learning experience, and one that will help him simply be himself on his next date.

AND FINALLY

Sometimes we find it hard to let go of old patterns because we're scared. The brain is made in such a way it is like a stuck record that keeps going round. But it doesn't have to be like that. You can stop it. We control our mind, not the other way around.

No one else can give you self-confidence. It has to come from inside you, and it comes from truly knowing yourself and what you are capable of. When we have self-confidence we can be anything we want to be – and do anything we want to do.

"

If you want to be loved, be lovable.

"

OVID

Arrival

Chapter Three

ON ENTERING THE LION'S DEN

Dates can be scary. I don't ever get nervous when I go on a date. If anything I feel excited. That's the best way to go into a date, but it is not always easy.

Of course the first thing people worry about is how they should greet each other, and the whole 'One kiss or two?' thing. It can feel uncomfortable. But if you are there first, simply stand up and smile and make an effort. If in doubt let them take the lead. The only rule? Definitely don't hug on the first date; it is a bit over-familiar.

People always tell me how nervous they are when they come into the *First Dates* restaurant, which is understandable. But sometimes that can come across as unappealing. If your date doesn't realize you're acting in an awkward way because of nerves, it can leave them thinking you're not interested, when actually you may fancy them like crazy. If you sit there with your arms crossed you are giving out a negative image. I know guarded body language often comes from a fear of rejection, but you have to take a chance.

We had a couple in the restaurant recently and they were awkward with each other. They didn't conform to the beauty 'ideal' that people see in magazines, and you could tell that both of them felt that. It was a shame, because they liked each other, but they had to spend quite a lot of time together before they started to relax and have fun. They were worried the other person was going to judge them before they even got to the table, rather than just waiting to see.

> 6 *If your date doesn't realize you're acting in an awkward way because of nerves, it can leave them thinking you're not interested.* 9

You need to get yourself into the right mindset and you should never walk into a date thinking that you're going to be judged, or thinking that you're lucky to be meeting that person. You should be thinking about how lucky they are to meet you. It is hard to exude confidence if you don't have it, but even things like talking to friends or family first can help to calm your nerves.

If someone is going on a date with an individual they don't know then they're already being very brave. They should feel proud. If you're training to be a boxer you don't fight in the world championship straight away. You have to be British champion, and then win the European belt and then you go to the world championship. If you take that same principle to dating you can work your way up to the big time. Don't think every date has to be a huge success. We are all learning as we go, and need to work our way up.

Eventually you will have enough experience to handle anyone, but don't expect to be an expert dater from the word go. The confidence will come. Just work on it until you make it. Smile as you walk in and keep telling yourself you are fine, and eventually you will believe it.

HOW WAS IT FOR YOU?

JODIE

'In my head I was thinking, "Why? Why did I say that? Don't show her all of your crazy straight away."'

First-time First Dater Jodie admits she was terrified about the idea of meeting a total stranger for dinner. But having been single for a year, the Newcastle native decided to take a leap of faith in the hope she would find someone who wasn't like her ex. 'My ex wasn't that nice to me even though we were together for eight years. I'm still not sure if that was love or Stockholm syndrome. I'd never been on a blind date in my life and I was drunk when I applied for the show. I was dead shocked when I was invited to go on but I knew it was time to meet someone nicer.'

Jodie had second thoughts minutes before arriving at the *First Dates* restaurant, but she managed to swerve a temptation. 'I passed a Sainsbury's on the way and I did think, "I could just go in there and get some food and go home." I needed a nervous wee. I was first to arrive and I was pleased, but there was still the whole "Do we hug or kiss?" dilemma to get over.'

Thankfully Jodie prepared for that first meeting with a little help from her friends. 'All my friends kept telling me to do different things – and I'm not very good at greeting people I don't know, as it is. I'd been building up for it for weeks and everyone's different when it comes to personal space, so I don't think there's a right or wrong answer. This may sound ridiculous but I did try a few different greetings with my friends. I'd make them walk towards me and practise giving them a hug or a kiss on the cheek to work out how it might go. I'd never met a potential girlfriend in such a formal way before because I usually just pull when I'm drunk. It's a two-way thing and I didn't know what my date would want to do. It was scary.'

After some soothing words from barman Merlin, 31-year-old Jodie was able to relax a little more. 'Arriving is scary, whatever happens, because of the fear of the unknown, but it's definitely best to be first. If you're second to arrive you're straight into the date and you don't have time to settle in. Arriving early also means you can clock your date before they clock you. I know people say you should go for personality but we're all a bit shallow and we do look at how hot someone is. I told myself that even if I didn't fancy my date I'd have a laugh. If there's one thing I can do, it's talk.'

So how did the big opener go? 'When my date, Laura, arrived she went in for a handshake and then a hug. It was a bit awkward but we got on well straight away. We had a good laugh over dinner but afterwards she put me in the friend-zone and said we were bantering more than flirting. I was hammered by that point so I got a bit upset. But at the end of the day not everyone fancies everyone else, do they?'

Not one to be put off easily, brave Jodie made a courageous return to the restaurant for another date with Louise. Having requested a mixture of Cheryl Cole and Katy Perry, she was elated when she got just that. 'I arrived first on the second date as well, which was a bonus. I promised myself not to get as drunk beforehand. I even said to Merlin, "I've got this, I'm not drunk." Then when Louise walked in she was fit as hell and I thought, "Oh my God, I wish I was more drunk." I wasn't sure what was coming out my mouth when she stood in front of me, because she was so stunning.'

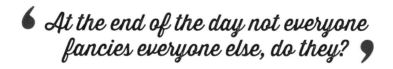

‘ At the end of the day not everyone fancies everyone else, do they? ’

It's fair to say that having been left speechless by Louise, Jodie's opening gambit didn't quite go to plan. 'I wanted to be cool but I was far from it. I wanted to give her a massive hug but instead I shook her hand. She looked at me a bit like, "Why are you doing that?" and it threw me off. Because I fancied her so much my head was all over the place and I felt dead self-conscious so I said something like, "Sorry about my stupid hair clip, I've got a cowlick and I have to try and pin it down." In my head I was thinking, "Why? Why did I say that? Don't show her all of your crazy straight away."'

Things picked up when the girls sat down to dinner, but sadly Perry-esque Louise decided she didn't feel fireworks with Jodie. 'That awful awkward first exchange is horrible and then it usually warms up, and it did but it took a little while. The conversation didn't flow as easily as it did with Laura, because Louise is much shyer, but we did have a nice time. She friend-zoned me after the meal, too. To be fair we have actually stayed friends, but I was disappointed.'

Currently single (and looking) postwoman Jodie has some helpful words of wisdom for people who are nervous about that big date arrival. 'One thing I will say if you're going on a date is don't be late. I'm always on time and often early. When people roll up really late and don't even try to apologize it sets a bad tone for the date in general. And don't get very drunk and cry like I did. That's never a good thing.'

SAM SAYS

Often, the most challenging part of a date is actually walking in because you've got so many things going through your head. 'What if they don't like me? What if I say something stupid? How should I greet them?'

You should just see how it goes when you're greeting someone. You might see them and think they're a handshake kind of person, or they might want to give you a massive hug, which will either break the ice or terrify you. The fact is we're talking about a few seconds of what will hopefully be a long date, so don't sweat if it fails to kick off like something out of a film.

I've had dates where it's been awkward for the first minute, but I always start asking questions straight away, even if it's just what the other person wants to drink. Once the conversation gets started it usually flows.

Jodie is one of my favourite *First Dates* characters. She seems confident and outgoing, but actually she was worried about both of her dates, which is why she had several drinks beforehand. Oh, and during the meal.

> ❛ *Often, the most challenging part of a date is actually walking in . . . Do whatever you can to make the other person feel at ease.* ❜

You'd feel comfortable with her straight away, because she's so chatty that you would never be stuck for something to talk about. She made the most of her dates and had a great time, even if they didn't end amazingly well. I felt bad for her when Laura and Louise gave her the 'friends' line, but I have no doubt she'll meet someone who adores her. The best bit of advice I could give about getting over nerves is just to go for it. And do whatever you can to make the other person feel at ease. Once you're both relaxed you can get on with the important job of having a brilliant night. Even if you don't fancy someone you can have a fantastic time and get to know them, and you may end up with a top mate.

UP CLOSE & PERSONAL

THE FROG TEST
SCOTT & CHARLI

Medical rep Scott, 29, is looking for 'a head turner' when she walks through the restaurant door, and for someone 'who doesn't take life too seriously'. He's already at the bar and quaffing a pint when 27-year-old make-up artist Charli arrives. Catching sight of this auburn beauty, with a striking emerald coat and matching frog bag, it's a wonder that Scott doesn't choke. Even Fred can't resist inquiring about her choice of accessory. 'It's just to see how guys react,' she says. Scott certainly can't ignore it when they're introduced, and the fact that he's charmed by Charli's quirky taste sets the stage for an engaging date.

HIGH HEELS, HIGH HOPES
LAURA & MATT

'Here she comes,' says Fred, on first sight of the tall blonde singleton as she approaches the restaurant. 'Oh my God! She can't walk.' Laura looks like a million dollars, and she'd practically float in like an angel if she wasn't struggling to stay upright in her towering stilettos. 'Is everything alright with your shoes?' Fred inquires when she finally totters through the door. 'They're too big for me,' wails Laura, but she's talking to a man who can help. Having escorted her to the bar stool, Fred sets about padding each shoe with folded strips of paper towel, so that by the time she's ready to join Matt at the table she crosses the floor with elegance and confidence.

THE MOMENT I SAW YOU
BRADLEY & LUCY

'I'm a little bit of a bossy-britches,' laughs Lucy, 26, from Manchester. She might arrive at the bar with bags of confidence, but for a moment that deserts her on hearing Fred welcome her date, Bradley, into the restaurant. 'I daren't look round,' she confesses to Merlin, staring hard at the bar. 'This is either the best or the worst idea I've ever had.' With no time to back out, Lucy turns to find she's about to share a table with a genuinely charming date. And though she's 'burned' at the end when Bradley admits that he doesn't feel that spark, Lucy leaves with no regrets.

BAR PRESENCE
RORY & MADDIE

Historical re-enactor Rory is first to arrive, and takes his seat at the bar. With time to kill ahead of his date with Aussie cross-stitcher Maddie, what better way to begin than by bonding with everyone's favourite cocktail king and conversation warm-up man? 'So, where are you from?' asks Merlin, on fulfilling Rory's request for a glass of water. 'Leicester,' he replies, before adding, 'I hate Leicester.' Rory goes on to explain that he grew up in South Africa. 'That must've been nice,' says Merlin, hoping to move their chat into more accommodating waters. 'No,' replies Rory, and scuppers that opportunity. A moment later, his date rocks up for the evening and Merlin politely takes the opportunity to give them some space.

AND FINALLY

No one ever achieved something by not trying. You should feel passion for everything you do in life. This way, in time, someone special will pay attention for all the right reasons.

Fear can be incredibly powerful, and it can hold us back from being and doing what we want. Once we break through that barrier it can make us feel like anything is possible. In my opinion, it is the only way we can truly experience what it means to be alive and in love.

"

*Well begun
is half done.*

"

ARISTOTLE

CICI

FROM:

Oxford

BEST DATE EVER:

It was just dinner, nothing special, but the conversation was so special we ended up knowing everything about each other.

WORST DATE EVER:

Sitting in absolute silence across the table from my date because neither of us knew what to say. Thankfully that was a long time ago.

FIRST KISS:

School disco, age 11, and it was disgusting.

CRUSH:

I'd have to go with Ryan Gosling.

PERFECT ROMANTIC NIGHT OUT:

It would start with coffee, with a shot of Baileys, and then a walk along the South Bank. We'd be holding hands and talking, or stopping to sit on a bench if we felt like it. We'd stop for food at some point, but nothing planned, and then a little bar hopping. Throughout, I'd want to feel completely involved with my date. You can probably tell I've thought about this quite a lot.

PERFECT ROMANTIC NIGHT IN:

Having dinner cooked for me while I watched my favourite movie with a glass of wine in hand.

GO-TO DATE OUTFIT:

Skinny jeans and a roll neck. Always black. Always heels.

EVER HAD A MISHAP AT THE RESTAURANT?

I'd been stuffing my face out the back, which I shouldn't have done, and came back with food trapped between my teeth. One of the customers spotted it. Mortifying.

FAVOURITE *FIRST DATES* COUPLE:

Frankie and Muhala

FUNNIEST *FIRST DATES* MOMENT:

Sam's ridiculously bad jokes.

WHAT HAS WORKING ON *FIRST DATES* TAUGHT YOU ABOUT LOVE?

Don't give up.

WHY SHOULD PEOPLE GO ON *FIRST DATES*?

To let us help you find love.

❝ Throughout, I'd want to feel completely involved with my date. You can probably tell I've thought about this quite a lot. ❞

Breaking the Ice

Chapter Four

THE ART OF BEING CHARMING

On the service course I run, I teach people that if you want to work to a good standard you must see, smile and say hello to people before they see, smile and say hello to you. It is your job to be charming first, not the other way around. The hospitality industry is a bit like dating, because it's about giving first and giving generously. When we talk about love it should always be better to give than to receive.

Some people are naturally charming, and for some people that art is learned. But once you learn it you have an indispensable skill for life. Once you know how to be polite and charming it can change your life.

I took my daughter to a restaurant in France that has an amazing reputation, but the waiters were all ignorant and rude. We sat there, disappointed. When our waiter came back over to take our order I asked his name and where he was from, taking a real interest in him. Suddenly he started to open up and smile. When he left the table my daughter said to me: 'Why is he being nice now when he wasn't before?' and I said, 'Because I was charming to him.' It was as simple as that.

If you are as charming as you can be, people will find it hard not to respond in the same way. To be charming you have to work at it.

First you need to know what other people want, and that is to be respected, understood and admired. There are dating rules in the animal kingdom and animals mate when they respond to each other. We need to be able to respond to each other and understand signs. People react to the eyes and they react to the senses. People have to like what they see, so smile. A smile is seen first in the eyes and then on the mouth, so it has to be genuine.

Sound is also very important, so the tone of your voice and how you articulate what you want to say means a lot. If the music is too loud somewhere you may have to shout to have a conversation. How can that be attractive? If you are somewhere that has soothing music it can make all the difference. Of course it is up to you what you like but John Holt and Gregory Isaacs always do it for me.

The important thing to remember is that you can be beautiful but not charming, and ugly but very charming. As long as you have a sexy attitude you can be incredibly attractive – no matter how you look. Sometimes the most beautiful people are the least charming because they don't feel like they have to make an effort. They rely solely on their looks, and eventually those looks may go.

If we all lived by the same principles, both people on a date would try and be charming. But some people don't bother and I just don't get it. How do they ever get anyone into bed? It must be alcohol. How terrible that someone has to be drunk to find you attractive.

> *As long as you have a sexy attitude you can be incredibly attractive – no matter how you look.*

The mind is every bit as important as how you look when it comes to meeting someone, if not more important. And so are kindness and understanding. Those things will win for me every time.

❦ HOW WAS IT FOR YOU? ❦

❧ **LUCY** ❧

'I blurted out, "I love you." Thankfully we laughed it off.'

Sometimes, no matter how much you want a date to work, it feels like Cupid is against you. When 29-year-old Lucy entered the *First Dates* restaurant, full of high hopes, she had no idea she was about to be the cause of her dining companion's wardrobe malfunction. 'I'd tried all of the usual methods of meeting people, like Tinder and Plenty of Fish, and it just wasn't happening. I love watching *First Dates*, and they've had some real successes, so I went for it. I was terrified actually walking into the restaurant because I was wearing wedges and I kept thinking I was going to fall over. I'd had a couple of drinks beforehand, which always helps, but not when you've got high shoes on.'

As the first to arrive Lucy got chatting to Merlin over a drink, and the barman was a little taken aback when this four-foot-eleven singleton revealed a surprising fact – she's an Olympic weightlifter. 'Merlin thought it was hilarious and asked if I could pick him up. I'm never one to shy away from a challenge so he walked round from behind the bar and I hauled him into the air. I'll never forget the look on Fred's face. That took my mind off how nervous I was, but I was still pretty terrified. I felt like I had to be careful of my facial expressions because it's so easy for your face to reveal whether you're excited or disappointed. You always want to make a good impression and those first moments are when you form an opinion of someone. When Caroline arrived I was happy, because she was very attractive, but we made a bit of a mess of the kiss, which wasn't ideal.'

After a slightly awkward start, the duo were soon chatting away over a cocktail, and discovered they had a lot of common ground. 'We were nervous but Caroline gave me a nice compliment and told me I looked lovely. We talked about the gym because she's into fitness too, and she said she often challenges dates to an arm-wrestle. But unfortunately instead of saying, "I love that idea," I blurted out, "I love you." Thankfully we laughed it off.'

Lucy didn't think the date could get much worse. But she was wrong. Very wrong. 'When Caroline heard I'd picked Merlin up she said she wanted to see if she could pick me up. We ended up in the middle of the bar area being stared at by other diners while she hoisted me up. To be fair she did a good job, but then suddenly the strap on her top broke and she was in serious danger of exposing herself to the rest of the restaurant.'

> ❛ *He walked round from behind the bar and I hauled him into the air.* ❜

It was Fred to the rescue when he rushed in with some black duct tape to reattach Caroline's strap. 'You couldn't make it up. Fred then whispered to her, "Don't worry, there's a panic button under the table." I think he thought I'd broken it on purpose. After that I decided that even if anything else went wrong it couldn't be as bad as ruining someone's outfit, so I might as well crack on and enjoy the date. We laughed about everything, so that broke the ice and all the tension disappeared, and after dinner we headed out to Soho for drinks.'

Just when the date was heading in the right direction, Caroline's friends turned up. 'Her mates were all nice people but the dynamic changed. I felt a bit like I was muscling in on Caroline's night with her friends, rather than enjoying a date. I don't know if the excitement of being in the restaurant wore off too, but the spark went and I made my excuses and left.'

Even though the evening hadn't gone as well as she'd hoped, Lucy decided she had nothing to lose in asking Caroline on another date. 'If you don't try, you don't know and all that. I sent her a text asking if she wanted to go climbing together, and made a silly joke about not staring at her bum. She messaged back saying, "Why don't we meet up as friends?" I totally got the friend card. But looking back, it was for the best. I've since met a girl on Tinder and it's going well.'

> ❛ *If something goes horribly wrong, the best thing to do is laugh about it and move on.* ❜

Not everyone can snap a date's top to break the ice, so what would Lucy suggest other nervous daters try? 'Talk! There's nothing worse than being on a date where it feels awkward. I've been on dates where the other person is really quiet so I've had to fill the dead air, and that can make things feel uncomfortable. One date didn't ask me any questions. Not a single one. And you kind of know if the conversation doesn't flow on a first date then it's not going to flow at all.'

Can she recommend any good ice-breaking subjects for a first date? 'I think talking about things like family and work is pretty easy because they're shared interests. We've all got families and jobs. But you need the other person to be involved in the conversation. If at any point you start thinking, "I don't know what to talk about," it's not a good sign. At the end of the day, you've just got to relax and enjoy a date. If something goes horribly wrong, the best thing to do is laugh about it and move on. It doesn't mean the date has to be a disaster. In fact, it can be positive.'

LAURA SAYS

Lucy and Caroline were amazing. From the moment they met we all had high hopes. There were just so many elements that matched up. They looked similar, mirrored each other's body language and broke the ice in every possible way.

Breaking the ice is all about that moment when you move from a formal introduction to something more personal and intimate. At the *First Dates* restaurant, this happens in so many ways, but it always begins with the introductory kiss. The fact is nobody knows what's acceptable – one kiss or two? Couples always end up in this awkward little shuffle, and sometimes talk it through by going, 'One, no? Oh . . . OK, two!' It makes me laugh every time, but we all do it, and I also think it helps to bring people together. You've shared your first awkward moment, after all.

Interestingly, Lucy and Caroline kept things quite formal after their introductory kiss, but not for long. They made small talk about their names, and then Lucy blurted out that she felt nervous. For me, that was the moment the ice started to crack. It's a confession, isn't it? You're taking your date into your confidence, admitting that you're only human, and basically hoping they feel the same way. Let's face it, that's not the kind of comment you make in a job interview. In a way ice-breakers exist to turn a formal situation into a chance to have fun. They serve an important purpose.

Then we had Caroline's strap crisis. When it comes to ice-breakers, this one sealed the deal. What started as a laugh could've ruined the date. Instead, it totally struck the right

> **❛ Nobody knows what's acceptable – one kiss or two? ❜**

note. From the moment Caroline realized she had snapped her shoulder strap in attempting to lift Lucy off her feet, I was ready for her to flee to the loos in tears. Instead she giggled, as did Lucy, before they both just fell about laughing. As Fred came to the rescue, they were like little kids who'd just done something naughty. That kind of moment unites people so well. Two relative strangers had found a way to connect.

Not all blind dates begin with the ice breaking in such a memorable way. Sometimes it can take a while to get beyond that formal phase. If you ever find yourself in that situation, and it feels like an interview with food, my advice is to keep chipping away. Sometimes it can take a lot of work to find a way through. It might be something neither of you plan, like a wardrobe malfunction, or an observation that gives you common ground. Often it just happens without either of you trying, which is why I find it best to just keep an open mind. And once you can relax in each other's company, that's when your personality can shine.

UP CLOSE & PERSONAL

NIGHT ON THE TILES
LOUIS & SOPHIE

'I've never actually been on a date before,' confesses sensitive wordsmith Louis, just moments before Sophie sweeps through the doors. 'But I want a relationship that all the poets wrote about in the past.' Facing each other at the bar, Louis calls upon his inner muse to kick off proceedings. 'I had a really fun day shopping for tiles,' he begins. 'Where did you go?' asks Sophie politely. 'Tile Land and Topps Tiles,' replies Louis, undergoing what must feel like a near-death-on-a-date experience. On the upside, the couple are quick to laugh at this cringeworthy cul-de-sac in conversation, which duly sets them on course for the sweetest of dates.

THE TOE CURL
ROBERT & AMY

Tattooed fifties fashionista Amy holds out hope that her date will prove to be 'someone a bit grown up, a bit nice and a bit gentlemanly'. As if made to order, in walks swinging sixties fan, Rob the Mod. He seems like an open-minded kind of guy, and so Amy does what every woman would do in her situation, and gets her cock out. When Rob lays eyes on the phallic symbol inked on her toe, it doesn't just break the ice but shatters it, and frees up this wonderful, good-humoured couple to properly get to know each other.

I GET KNOCKED DOWN
ROSS & SARAH-JAYNE

Ross is back for his third date at the restaurant. Warrington teacher Sarah-Jayne is also on a return attempt to find love, and so this is a big moment for them both. Ross has never heard a Warrington accent, as he remarks when she takes her seat. Sarah-Jayne eyes him warily, unsure whether to be offended. She opts to start again by reaching across the table to shake his hand, only to tip over a wine glass. 'That was your fault,' says Ross, which is a heart-stopping moment and the perfect opportunity for the couple to dissolve into giggles. It doesn't lead to true romance, but the pair enjoy a lot of laughs in discovering they're not made for each other.

PARTY ON
BERTIE & BELLA

The moment ex-public schoolboy Bertie sets eyes on Bella at the bar, he seems a little lost for words. It's no surprise, in view of the latex-clad vision set to share a table with him. Politely Bertie keeps his eyes from popping out on stalks, and inquires after Bella's interests. 'Fun, crazy things,' she tells him very simply. 'Who doesn't love a party?' In response, Bertie lets his composure slip. 'Oh, I love a party,' he tells her with a hint of mischief and a wicked smile. 'I think we're going to get on.'

⚬—⚬ AND FINALLY ⚬—⚬

A smile can be the beginning of something incredible. A warm greeting and kindness is something that money cannot buy. You can be a millionaire and shower someone with gifts, but a simple compliment is worth so much more.

Charm is not about how handsome or beautiful you are, but how handsome or beautiful you can make yourself by being a good and respectful person. The most physically beautiful person in a room can be the least charming, and that is the impression they make on us. Manners cost nothing but they are priceless.

"

Fortune favours the bold.

"

VIRGIL

DATE LINES . . .

THEY SAID
WHAT?

Find out who's behind these quotes
on page 251

1. 'When I dance, it's like having an orgasm'

2. 'I'll be 26 in two weeks'
   'Yeah? I thought you were older'
   'Do I look older?'

3. 'Just getting my calculator out . . . you had more of the brownie'

4. 'Why would I kiss 100 frogs 'cause I know they're frogs? I'd rather wait out for my prince'

5. 'I'm so emotional that I can fall in love with anyone at any time'

6. 'I'm ready to slay the males'

7. 'I don't think happiness lies with being a lesbican (sic). I need a man to look after me'

8. 'I actually write a dating blog'
   'Oh, my Lord . . . OK'

9. 'I'm actually looking at your eyes'
   Closes eyes: 'What colour are they?'
   'I'm just looking at your boobs now your eyes are closed'

10. 'My first dates don't usually consist of food'

11. 'I'm not really in a place for bread at the moment'

Building the Bond

ON MAKING CONNECTIONS THAT MATTER

To really connect with someone you need to make them feel good. Paying compliments is very important. It can be the subtlest thing but it will make someone feel at ease. It takes a little and means a lot.

If you want to forge a connection with someone you must give them your undivided attention and be able to focus on what they are saying without any distractions. There's nothing worse than someone going for a date and then sitting and looking at their phone the entire time. You are basically telling someone they are not very interesting if you are looking at Twitter constantly.

There have been people in the restaurant who get to the end of their dates and they don't even know each other's names because they're not concentrating one bit. You can go home and spend all night looking at Facebook on your iPad if you want to, but for that time you're on the date you should be completely attentive.

Listening and observing go together, and not judging people goes hand in hand with that. Remember that the person you're with is as nervous as – if not more nervous than – you, so they may say the wrong thing sometimes.

If your date is talking about something you don't understand, try and take something from that conversation, even if it's only tiny. If it is important to them it should be important to you. And if you do not understand something, ask them about it and engage with them.

Trust is an important thing even before a relationship starts. In religion trust is the basis of love, and therefore without trust there is no love. How do you know if there is trust? First of all you must trust yourself. I once read that chemistry can only happen between two people who are good. Socrates held the pursuit of virtue as the meaning of life, and that means knowing what is good and knowing what is bad. Being good is not easy to define but in my opinion it is about being honest, kind, generous and having empathy for others. If you don't have a good heart how can you feel love?

To have a good heart you have to accept you will do things wrong sometimes, and make amends when you do. If you trust yourself to do the right thing, you can trust others too.

> 6 *If you don't have a good heart how can you feel love?* 9

My son drew a ladder the other day but there were some rungs missing from it and I said to him, 'How can you expect to get all the way to the top if you're missing rungs?' It is the same with love. You need to have all the steps in place to get to the top so it works. One of those steps is trust, and another is kindness. Be as kind as you can be, and it will always come back to you.

HOW WAS IT FOR YOU?

ARUNIMA

'As soon as I saw Simon, I thought, "Everything is going to be OK."'

The first to arrive in the restaurant, Arunima gave no thought as to what her date might look like. Waiting at the table, glancing nervously at the door, the 29-year-old lawyer's sole concern was how he would react to her. 'No matter who came in,' she said, 'I just didn't know whether my wheelchair would be an issue for them. It's a blind date, after all. As a result, I had to be ready for that person to take one look at me and walk out again. I didn't want them to be disappointed, or feel that I had failed to live up to their expectations.'

Thanks to dating apps, the prospect of meeting a stranger for dinner is softened by the fact that you can build a picture of each other beforehand. Without this comfort blanket, Arunima found she had to place a great deal of trust in a man who knew nothing about her. 'This is where the seed of the bond began,' she explains. 'Even before we'd met, I had to feel like he was someone who would accept me as I am. That was key to me being there in the first place.'

Arunima decided on a whim to give this blind date a shot. In the past, she admits, the kind of guys she'd been involved with romantically always needed 'rescuing' by her and never thrived as a result. 'I wanted someone stable, and capable of holding a good conversation,' she says. 'I just hadn't had much luck in finding him.' Arunima credits her friends for encouraging her out of her comfort zone and into the *First Dates* restaurant. Even as she waited at her table with nothing but uncertainty for company, she knew it had been the right thing to do. 'Without my mates, I'd have stayed at home,' she laughs. 'I've lived with disability my whole life, and it's friends and family who give me that confidence to try new things. While I'm the sort of person who needs that nudge, I also know that once I'm in a new situation I can take care of myself.'

When veterinary surgeon Simon, 27, joined her, Arunima responded with a silent *Yippee*! 'He just looked lovely,' she says. 'He was handsome, polite, and had such warm, friendly eyes. There was a vibe about him that I found really attractive. In fact, as soon as I saw Simon, I thought, "Everything is going to be OK."'

It's one thing to get a sense that your date has a good heart, which was critical for Arunima to feel at ease. But even with a decent first impression, how do two strangers set about building a bond? 'I'm a naturally honest person,' she explains. 'So I tend to blurt out whatever I'm feeling. When Simon joined me, the first thing I did was tell him how scared I felt. I remember those words coming out of my mouth, but I also thought that if I can be this open about myself then maybe it'll help him to be honest with me. We were going through a shared experience, after all. We each had our own insecurities and objective in being there, and it gave us something in common. As soon as I opened up, he did the same,' she finishes. 'It formed a thread between us.'

As for the moment when that thread began to strengthen and grow, Arunima can pinpoint the moment precisely. 'Our first laugh,' she says simply. 'I told him his dog should've joined us for the date, which was such a silly idea but it made us both giggle. All of a sudden, we'd moved beyond formal small talk into something special. Soon after that I demonstrated the horn fitted to my chair, and things just took off from there.'

While laughter marked a defining moment on the date, Arunima found herself tuning into other signs that the couple were bonding. 'Eye contact was easy with Simon,' she says. 'It didn't feel forced or awkward, and nor did our conversation. I was able to listen to what he had to say, rather than worry about what I was going to offer next. It flowed naturally, and that just helped us both to relax. In a way,' she adds, when describing how it felt to be in Simon's company, 'it reminded me of that moment when you settle into bed at the end of a long day. All the weight falls off your shoulders, and you can just be yourself.'

To understand the importance of a bond on any date, romantic or otherwise, how would Arunima have responded had she not clicked with Simon? 'I'd have been a tense hedgehog,' she chuckles. 'Very prickly and hard to get to know. But as I felt so at ease in his company, it meant I could let my personality unfold. Thanks to Simon, I was free to enjoy being a girl on a regular date, rather than someone in a wheelchair who was worried about what people think of her.'

The bond forged between Simon and Arunima was clear for everyone to see, and proved to be one of the most touching and empowering of all the encounters on *First Dates*. But where did the connection take them? Arunima smiles philosophically. 'There was nothing romantic there,' she admits. 'It didn't need spelling out, but then I genuinely felt like I had found a true friend. That was enough to leave me on cloud nine as we left. Love comes in many forms, after all, and not just from a relationship. So it felt awesome that I was lucky enough to have met someone who understood me and enjoyed being in my company just as much. That's not a bond based on whether they can walk as well as you or anything like that. It's all about the heart and mind.'

As well as sharing a passion for animals during their date, Arunima also confessed to being an unrepentant bingo fan. While it tickled Simon over dinner, did he ever live up to his promise to join her for an evening out with her senior ladies? 'He totally did and now he's chasing that win,' Arunima confirms. 'He's even texted me since to ask if we can go again. I haven't introduced him to my posse yet, but I'm sure I will in due course. He'll need their sign-off before he can sit with us,' she points out with a twinkle in her eye. 'Then the transition will be complete.'

> ❛ *I was free to enjoy being a girl on a regular date.* ❜

CICI SAYS

People are naturally nervous when they arrive in the *First Dates* restaurant, but Arunima was also one of the friendliest I've ever met. All the staff agreed that she had an aura about her. She was like this bright spirit, full of life and energy, and we adored her.

As a waitress, I see couples forming bonds all the time. From a personal perspective, I find eye contact is the critical factor. It's something we all do when we're genuinely interested in someone, because we're listening to what they have to say or expressing things we'd like them to understand. It's a natural instinct, I think. It can't be faked, and that was evident in the way Simon and Arunima related to one another.

I'm a big believer in looking for visual indicators that you're making a connection. Then again, there's always a chance that you can become aware of how you're coming across. It means you might switch things on or censor yourself accordingly. Both Simon and Arunima seemed natural in that respect, but above all it was the flow of conversation that told me how well they were getting along. Sometimes, when that bond just isn't happening, you'll find people literally looking to the staff for help. They'll call us across with questions about the menu, place an order for the sake of it, or even ask permission to visit the loo. Simon and Arunima didn't once waver; there were also lots of smiles and laughter coming from their table. I always assume this must mean love is in the air, but Sam isn't quite so convinced. He thinks people often do that to be polite, but we both agree that if a bond is going to develop into something romantic then flirting has to come into play.

While their date didn't lead to romance, Simon and Arunima left having become firm friends. There was no need for them to put that into words. It was apparent in the way they'd found each other across the table. That kind of bond is just as valid as one that brings you together with a partner for life. It's also worth noting that any kind of meaningful connection is something that develops and strengthens over time. Whether you've met your soulmate or a person who you'd simply like to be part of your life on some level, it's a precious thing, and I'm thrilled that Arunima found that in our restaurant.

UP CLOSE & PERSONAL

BEYOND THE BEARD
LIAM & KATE

When trainee midwife Kate lays eyes on trainee paramedic Liam, she does her best to ignore the elephant in the room. The couple seem well suited, and yet their chatter flows in every direction but one. For Liam is blessed with the finest ginger facial hair in South London. The auburn adventurer look has brought him attention from women in the past, but our man jokes beforehand that it 'makes him feel cheap'. Instead, as the conversation deepens, he opens up about his happy childhood with two mums. While Kate is genuinely interested, eventually she caves. 'OK,' she says, 'we need to talk about your beard.' The evening doesn't end in romance, but here is a couple that made an effort getting to know each other and enjoyed every moment.

A DEEPER UNDERSTANDING
ALEX & JSKY

Alex, 29, describes herself as a straight girl in a boy's body. She's self-assured and glamorous, and proud of her identity. So when her date walks in with earrings the size of basketball hoops, it seems she's set to meet a guy who also likes to express his individuality. They might come from different backgrounds, but their journeys provide common ground. It doesn't dominate their conversation, but offers each of them insights they wouldn't get by sticking at small talk. With dinner over, both Alex and Jsky are keen to find out more about each other, and head off into town in search of a drink and a place to keep talking.

PASSION FOR PUGS
GARETH & SUZIE

Finding common ground with a stranger can be a challenge for some, but not pug-mad Suzie. She's arrived at the restaurant concerned that her passion might put off her date. Fortunately, Gareth has a lot to offer in terms of personality and charm, which makes the small talk run smoothly. Then he drops in that he's had to walk his dog before heading out to join her, and Suzie's attention spikes. 'What kind of dog do you have?' she asks. Gareth looks a little embarrassed, possibly wishing he owned something more manly, but opts for an honest answer. 'Shut up! You've actually got a pug?' she shrieks as her expression brightens by a thousand watts.

THE FORCE IS STRONG
LACHLAN & RACHEL

Web developer Lachlan craves a girl who will 'accept me for the nerd I am', but he's convinced that's a tall order. Sure enough, on meeting drop-dead-gorgeous psychologist Rachel, it does look like one of them has wandered into the wrong dating division. Lachlan holds his own, however, and truly shines when he dares to express his devotion to *Star Wars*. Not only is Rachel a fan, he discovers to his astonishment, but she's just as passionate about ranking the movies from best to worst. While this alliance of minds doesn't lead to romance, Lachlan and Rachel swap numbers outside the restaurant as firm friends. When the next instalment of everyone's favourite intergalactic saga hits our screens, she can be sure to expect a call.

AND FINALLY

In order to connect with others we must first connect with ourselves. Love and trust are about acceptance of both yourself and everyone else.

Building a bond takes time because trust needs to be established first, and that is done through talking and sharing, and being our true selves. When someone loves you, they don't love you because you're perfect. They love you in spite of the fact that you're not.

*You cannot open
a book without
learning something.*

CONFUCIUS

Show & Tell

Chapter Six

THE BIG REVEAL

There is such a thing as a 'need to know' basis, and therefore there are some conversations which are not meant for a first date.

I would suggest only telling people what they need to know and keeping some things back for when you feel more confident or you trust them more. It doesn't mean that you're lying or you're not trustworthy, you're just not sharing everything about yourself. And why should you? Until you decide you are happy revealing secrets about yourself, they are just for you.

We have to be smart and strategic and know that not all truths are to be shared straight away. It is all about timing. We have to put ourselves in other people's shoes and realize that they may not be ready to cope with our life story.

Some people who have come into the restaurant have been very open and honest, and I applaud that. If they have a big secret they feel like they want to share it straight away, whether they've been through a divorce, or they're asexual or transgender. All of those things have happened here, and the people involved have chosen to tell people from the word go because it is important to them.

Now, these are the kind of big admissions that perhaps you should be upfront about. But when it comes to chatting about ex-partners, for example, I would exercise caution. There is a time and place to talk in detail about past relationships, and it is not the first time you meet someone. No one wants to hear about how your ex cheated on you or broke your heart when you're trying to have a fun evening. First dates should be about laughter and lightness, and later dates are for sharing more.

When it comes to conversations in general, I don't think you want to get too caught up in what to talk about. Why? Because conversations need to flow. You should take it as it comes, but equally there is no harm in having ideas for things to talk about if the conversation falls flat. You could find yourself talking about things you're not comfortable with to fill the silence, and that's when any skeletons that are hiding in your closet can spill out.

> *First dates should be about laughter and lightness, and later dates are for sharing more.*

Honesty is very important in a relationship in general but what if I wish to do something and I'm not sure if the other person will like it? Should I tell them? If I am in any doubt, I will always wait until I get to know them better. You don't want to bombard people with too many revelations at once.

⤨ HOW WAS IT FOR YOU? ⤪

⤳❃ **RICHARD** ❦⤲

'I just took the plunge and said, "There's one thing you may find interesting about me . . ."'

So, you're enjoying a blind date, and slowly getting to know each other. Things are looking good, but there's something about yourself that you feel the need to share if things are going to develop further.

The trouble is you've no idea how this person is going to react, and it could make or break the date.

For Richard, a level-headed 20-year-old Oxford student, the prospect of telling musical-theatre enthusiast Freya about his asexuality wasn't something that he felt ready for. 'I wasn't even sure if I was going to bring it up at all,' he admits, referring to the fact that he lives happily with no sexual desire. 'It's clearly a part of my identity,' he explains, 'but I don't feel it defines me as a person. We all have lots of elements that come together in a bundle to constitute who we are, and so I didn't want to sit down and make it a front-line thing.'

While Richard feels no sexual attraction to people of either gender, he does experience an interest in romance with the opposite sex. Through his eyes, the *First Dates* restaurant provided an ideal opportunity for him to seek that connection. 'I was drawn by the diversity of people that go there,' he explains. 'It can also be a very honest environment, and so I decided there would be no harm in giving it a shot. In the build-up to the date, I tried not to prejudge who I might be paired with. Of course I hoped to find someone of a similar age who shared my interests. If I was going to open up to this person then it was really important to have that common ground. At the same time, my mystery date was pretty much a fictional character in my mind. Then I arrived, everything became very real, and the nerves kicked in.'

Blind dates can be testing at the best of times, but how does it feel to go in knowing there's an aspect of your life that might change everything if you share it? 'It's always difficult to tell how someone will react,' says Richard candidly. 'I never feel sure about that, which is why it's important that I go in feeling confident. This is the basis from which to form bonds with people,' he continues. 'It means knowing your own foibles as much as anything else. While you don't want to pretend to be someone completely different, and you should have no sense of shame about who you really are, it's about presenting yourself in the most attractive light to make a good first impression. This way, they can get to know you a little bit before you think about sharing deeper, more personal aspects of your life.'

Even before they'd left the bar for the table, it was evident to one and all that Richard and Freya would get on famously. Soon after meeting his song-and-dance-loving date, Richard had serenaded her with a line from his own showstopper, a satirical composition called *UKIP: The Musical*. 'We had a lot in common,' he says with a smile, 'and so it helped me to get a sense of whether my asexuality would be an issue, or if it was something so new that Freya would need a lot of time to process it.'

Every date is different, of course, but is there ever a good moment to put that person in the picture? 'We were talking about our relationship experience,' says Richard, 'and in that context it felt like relevant information. To put it another way, it seemed to me to be a deception by omission if I didn't bring it up. Even so, the precise timing was unclear to me until I just took the plunge and said, "There's one thing you may find interesting about me . . ." Then, once I'd started, there was no going back. I had to just come out with it.'

To Richard's relief, Freya simply took the news in her stride. But is there ever a risk that revealing too much about yourself can dominate the rest of the date? 'Of course,' Richard agrees. 'Which is why it's good to prepare the way beforehand by getting to know each other as much as you can. It makes it easier to place everything into context. Yes, I'm asexual, but it doesn't govern my life. It's just one aspect of who I am that I chose to share with Freya so she could get a better understanding of me. A good rule of thumb is to ask yourself if you're ready to handle any reaction, and recognize that if it doesn't go well that says more about the other person than it does about you. In my case,' he says, 'Freya appreciated my openness and I appreciated her positive reaction. Revealing something so personal is a core part of bonding with someone, and it helped us to enjoy the rest of the date. It was a significant moment for sure, but we soon moved on to other topics. For me, once it was in the open I could relax.'

No doubt it takes courage to be so frank with a relative stranger. How would he have felt had he chosen to stay quiet? 'It would've taken the sheen off our date,' he says. 'We had a connection but, by not telling her, that would've become precarious had things developed. I would've had to tell her at some point, without knowing how she'd respond, and that takes away an element of security. Of course, if there'd been no connection at all then I might've kept it to myself. There's no iron law about how much to reveal on a first date. But I went ahead because I believe the act of sharing something so personal shows that you rate that person. You're taking them into your trust with sensitive information, and hoping they'll respond with respect.'

> **❛ Revealing something so personal is a core part of bonding with someone. ❜**

Richard successfully negotiated sharing an intimate aspect of his life with Freya, but did it lead to love? 'We genuinely had a nice evening,' he says, 'but despite the connection I think we both felt there was no romantic spark. Even so, I'm profoundly grateful to Freya for being such great company, and I learned that even relative strangers can be remarkably accepting. I put myself on the line, but it was worth it. Ultimately, blind dating is fun,' he declares with a grin. 'You go to dinner with someone you know nothing about and then trade information about each other over the course of an evening. But you don't just build up a picture of that person. You learn a great deal about yourself.'

SAM SAYS

I'm one hundred per cent for people being themselves on dates; I don't think you should ever put on a show. But I also think that you don't want to tell someone absolutely everything about yourself on a first date. The deeper things should be saved for later on down the line, when you're ready.

Richard was incredibly brave to tell Freya that he was asexual on their first date, and obviously he felt like that was the right time for him. It's a personal choice and some people may think it's a big thing to tell someone something that personal early on, but others may be more comfortable getting everything out in the open.

You can only tell if it's the right time to share when you're on the date, because you can kind of gauge how someone will react when you've spent some time in their company. If you know you don't want to see someone again there's no need to open up to them, but if you do it's best to be upfront about something that could be a game changer.

You should keep yourself open to what people are going to say on dates. If someone has got a story to tell there's a reason why they're choosing to share it. It can't be easy to be that honest with a stranger, so concentrate on what they're saying and keep an open mind. And listen! Make sure your date has all your attention, because it's very obvious if someone is only half interested.

Often people over-share when they're nervous or drunk. I definitely talk too much on dates sometimes, and I've been guilty of sharing too much too early. I tend to go off at a tangent and forget why I started the conversation, and that can be distracting for the other person. My default is to ask someone about where they live if I go off track. That's what I always fall back on.

UP CLOSE & PERSONAL

REALITY CHECK
PAUL & SAMANTHA

Paul, 30, drops a bit of a bombshell when he meets his date, 24-year-old Samantha. 'I'm going to put it out there,' he says, before she's barely had a sip of her drink. 'I used to be a woman.' Samantha forgets to blink for a moment. There's no issue for her, but it's a massive surprise so early on, along with his bonus revelation that his new parts are fully functional. Having no idea that Paul is joking Samantha looks for common ground. 'These aren't real,' she says, pointing to her chest. 'What aren't?' asks Paul playfully. 'The old Barrys,' says Samantha, before this couple head for their table to properly get to know each other.

THE HEEL BOMB
PAOLO & DANIEL

Navigating his way through the gay dating scene hasn't been easy for Paolo, a Catholic boy from small-town Italy. He looks magnificent, and from where similarly bearded companion Daniel is sitting it's evidently appreciated. They're getting to know each other, and both like what they see. Eventually, Paolo feels ready to reveal himself in full – by showing Daniel a picture of himself in eleven-inch heels. While Daniel might consider himself to be open-minded, this is a step too far for him. Within minutes, poor Paolo has asked for the bill.

THE INTERVIEW
JAYDEN & ISABEL

When it comes to how much you reveal about yourself on a first date, a great deal rests on how comfortable you feel in the company of a stranger. Jayden doesn't have that luxury, however. While Isabel's clearly interested in him, she has a list of direct personal questions and expects instant, honest answers. 'So, are you looking for someone?' she asks, easing him in gently. Jayden responds politely, and confirms that he is. 'Are you a virgin?' she inquires to follow, and the poor young man almost chokes. Despite such a probing inquiry, during which it's a surprise that Isabel doesn't ask to see a relationship CV, Jayden handles himself terrifically. Ultimately, in spite of his efforts, Isabel chooses not to award him the role of second-date companion.

THIS IS ME
CHUKS & GRACE

By her own admission, 28-year-old arts administrator Grace doesn't date a lot. For someone with little experience of seeking a connection with strangers, she's a natural in Chuks' company, and the couple quickly feel at ease with one another. Over drinks and dinner, they talk about every subject under the sun, peppered with lots of heartfelt laughter. By dessert, it's quite clear that something special is happening here, and yet the fact that Chuks lives with a physical disability is neither here nor there. He feels no obligation to address it because, frankly, it's irrelevant. 'I couldn't have been matched with someone better,' says Grace afterwards, before happily agreeing to a second date.

AND FINALLY

I am very much for people being open and honest, but there is a line! Over-sharing is more dangerous than not sharing enough. You may never see this person again, and so do you really want them knowing personal things about you?

Don't feel any pressure to tell people everything about yourself. You can be fun and entertaining without sharing too much private information. There are so many things you can talk about other than yourself, and it is always nice to keep some things back for later on.

"
No legacy is so rich as honesty.
"

WILLIAM SHAKESPEARE

ALL'S WELL THAT ENDS WELL

MERLIN

FROM:

London

BEST DATE EVER:

With my girlfriend in Goa, India. We found a completely deserted beach and had some beautiful food while we watched the sun set. It was very romantic.

WORST DATE EVER:

It wasn't even a date as such but I met a girl when I sat next to her at a party. The first thing she said to me was, 'Shall we get a cab?' We ended up going out for six months.

FIRST KISS:

I honestly can't remember but I know it will have been awkward. It's never the perfect moment you want it to be.

CRUSH:

I haven't got one. I don't keep up with celebrity culture so I don't know who anyone is!

PERFECT ROMANTIC NIGHT OUT:

A good meal in a nice mainland European city in summer. And then on for a flutter and a cocktail in a casino.

PERFECT ROMANTIC NIGHT IN:

I do like my food so it would involve cooking something nice, and then my girlfriend and I like to play backgammon. It sounds weird but playing board games is a really social thing to do.

GO-TO DATE OUTFIT:

If we were going to a formal restaurant it would be a three-piece suit and a good pair of shoes. If you're wearing that, you can go anywhere.

EVER HAD A MISHAP AT THE RESTAURANT?

I once asked a big rugby player sat at the bar what kind of girl he was hoping to meet and he replied, 'I'm meeting a guy, actually.' You can never judge a book by its cover. I ask people outright now if they're meeting a guy or a girl.

FAVOURITE *FIRST DATES* COUPLE:

Adam and Dan. They're absolutely tremendous, and they're the nearest thing I get to regulars because they're always in and out.

FUNNIEST *FIRST DATES* MOMENT:

We had a guy in for a date and one of the crew told me he looked really familiar. I asked him if he'd been on TV before and it turned out he was a porn star.

WHAT HAS WORKING ON *FIRST DATES* TAUGHT YOU ABOUT LOVE?

That there really is someone for everyone. The more shows we do the more I know it's true. Also, that you can't judge anyone from how they look because people will always surprise you.

WHY SHOULD PEOPLE GO ON *FIRST DATES*?

It's a lot of fun, you've got nothing to lose and it's a great place to look for the person of your dreams. *First Dates* has got an amazingly professional team matching people and having brilliant success.

Body Language

Chapter Seven

ON READING BETWEEN THE LINES

Body language is incredibly important when you're first meeting someone. Your date will be constantly picking things up from the way you sit, stand and even where you place your arms. They may not even be conscious of it, but your body is telling them so many things.

You need to be very aware of what your body language says when you first meet your date. Will they be able to tell if you're not very keen? Will they know you want to get them into bed? Probably. Sometimes what we don't say is what speaks the loudest.

I see it all the time in the restaurant. People greet each other as if they're terrified, and that is not a great way to start a date. The best thing to do is to greet people warmly and tell them how much you've been looking forward to meeting them.

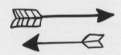

Suggest you get a drink, and ask if they've seen the menu. Maybe you can look at the menu together. That way you're on common ground and it brings you a bit closer together physically. It is a very inoffensive topic but it can yield a long conversation about what food you do and don't like and forge an initial connection so you feel more relaxed. When you feel relaxed, your body will tell your date exactly that.

Of course it goes without saying that if you sit there with your arms crossed you are giving out a negative image. I know that kind of approach often comes from a fear of rejection because some people are worried they won't be liked, but you have to give them a chance to get to know you first. Otherwise they will only be rejecting a guarded, closed version of you.

> *When you feel relaxed, your body will tell your date exactly that.*

People will even be reading the way you walk when you arrive at the date. If you're there first it is easier because you can sit down and have a drink while you wait. But if you are the person who arrives second you are more on show. So walk with pride and remember how wonderful you are. First impressions are so important. It doesn't mean the date is going to be a disaster if you don't make a good entrance, but it is nice to start off on a positive footing.

A small thing like touching someone on the arm when you're talking shows you're listening and taking an interest. Of course you only want to do that if you're flirting, so you don't give someone the wrong impression, but being tactile is a sure sign that you like someone. I'm not talking about stroking someone's leg under the table here. Subtlety is the key.

❧ HOW WAS IT FOR YOU? ❧

❧ **BECKY** *❧*

'Being face-to-face with someone makes it so much easier to work out if there's something between you.'

As a dancer and teacher, 28-year-old Becky from Hertfordshire considers herself to be body literate. 'I specialize in burlesque, which is an all-encompassing celebration of the female form,' she says. 'Performing helps me to feel confident and sassy, and I try to bring that into a dating situation.'

In an age where apps enable couples to connect, Becky was drawn to the *First Dates* restaurant because she felt it offered something that had become lost in recent times: the chance to interact with someone up close and personal right from the start. 'I was attracted to the physical aspect,' she explains. 'Actually sitting across the table from someone tells you so much more about them than anything they might write on a screen. Online dating is great, but sometimes you can come across someone and think you have something going between you. Then you meet for real, get a chance to read their body language, and discover that spark is missing. There's also something very romantic about the prospect of a blind date in a candlelit restaurant,' she adds. 'It's a sweet and genuine means of dating, and I really hoped I might find love there.'

So, in the world of body language, what elements speak volumes? 'Eye contact,' says Becky without hesitation. 'It can be quite intimidating when you're facing a stranger, but you can tell a great deal about how someone is feeling simply by holding their gaze.' There is a fine line, of course, between looking at someone with interest as you chat, and simply staring – nobody wants to come across like a potential serial killer. Becky points out that it's just one of many visual elements that contribute to the flow of the date. 'Smiles are important because they generate warmth,' she says, 'but in general it's about being open and relaxed in a physical way. If you're closed off, from not maintaining eye contact to folding your arms, that gives off a clear vibe and makes it very hard for the other person to find a way in.'

So, in a dating situation, is Becky conscious of her own body language? 'I try to be very open as a person. I put things out there about my life so they can make decisions about whether they want to get involved with me. I do feel that's reflected in the way I come across physically,' she says, 'but I try not to think about it too much. It isn't something you can fake, after all.'

Becky's belief that couples need to meet for real in order to work out if they're compatible came true on her first visit to the restaurant. On paper, comedian Lewis should've put a big smile on her face. While Becky is quick to stress that she found her date to be thoroughly decent, the chemistry just wasn't there. 'Lewis seemed quite nervous to me, not just in his conversation but his manner. I tried to put him at ease,' she says before reflecting for a moment, 'but I think that might've just been a little overwhelming.'

While both Becky and Lewis recognized they just weren't meant to be, neither one spelled it out verbally. 'If you were to watch our date again,' she suggests, 'and turn the volume down, it's evident from our body language that it wasn't working out. I certainly wasn't as open or as flirtatious as I might've been. It just wasn't the kind of date where I'd be playing with my hair or offering a cheeky smile. I just tried to make him feel comfortable so we could enjoy our meal.'

Undeterred, Becky returned to the restaurant in the hope that she might find someone 'with more of an edge'. What she got, with just once glance at the heavily inked man who arrived on time, caused her to giggle with excitement. 'John's physical appearance instantly intrigued me,' she explains, on reliving the moment her tattooist date joined her at the bar. 'He was obviously very confident in his own skin, and I identified with that. He was also a natural with his conversation. It helped me to feel relaxed, but I also might've read too much into that side of things.'

While the date went well for the couple, peppered with laughter and chat about John's private piercings, Becky can't help but sound disappointed that romance failed to blossom afterwards. She acknowledges that it's very easy to look back on any date and see things in a clearer light, but now believes she missed one vital sign that John didn't share her affections. 'We got along so well that I stopped paying attention to his body language,' she says. 'When I watched our date back, I realized he was leaning away from me while I was leaning in. Had I registered that at the time, it wouldn't have come as such a surprise when nothing came of our time in the restaurant.'

Cupid's arrow might've missed Becky on both occasions, but she came away from the experience with the firm belief that face-to-face dating is the surest way of finding a soulmate. 'Don't do everything over the Internet,' she says, when asked what advice she would give anyone else in the dating game. 'Go out and meet people for real. It takes a bit of courage to put yourself in that position, but being face-to-face with someone makes it so much easier to work out if there's something between you.'

While Becky's quest to find 'the One' continues, there's no doubt in her mind that body language speaks louder than words. 'Even if you feel you're getting on really well with that person,' she continues, 'make sure you pay attention to those visual signs. The way they present themselves physically can be deeply revealing about what's really going on in both their heart and mind.'

Don't do everything over the Internet . . . Go out and meet people for real.

LAURA SAYS

When she arrived at the restaurant, I could tell Becky was a confident woman. She carried herself well, with a striking look to back it up. While her date, Lewis, was a lovely guy, he didn't seem at ease, and this set the tone for their time together. Serving the tables, it's often very clear how things are working out between a couple just by looking at how they're sitting. Sadly, neither of them could get beyond polite conversation, and that's when Becky eased off in the physical sense. It was this shift in her manner that told me the date was heading for the friend-zone.

To give them both credit, facing a stranger across a table can be an intense experience. When things are genuinely good, couples lean in with smiles and a sparkle in their eyes. If things have failed to take off then it can literally look like they're trying to get away from each other. I'll always remember one guy who was leaning so far back in his chair I thought he was going to topple over.

Becky says she only realized that her second date, John, wasn't quite as keen as she had believed when she watched their time together on TV. It's very easy in hindsight to spot those telltale indicators, like crossing hands protectively or breaking eye contact, but when you're in that moment it's tough. That's why I think she's being a little hard on herself when she says she should've seen it coming. I genuinely thought that romance was in the air when Becky and John visited us. It just so happened that she was in the company of a charming guy who could make good conversation. She got swept up in all the signs that suggested he shared her interest, focusing on the chat and the banter over the body language, and so understandably it came as a disappointment to her to learn that she'd been wide of the mark.

It's certainly useful to note your date's body language, but from your side of the table you don't want to get too focused on how you're coming across. The moment you start to think about it, you stop being natural. It's so important to be yourself, even if it isn't working out for you, so you can present a truthful picture. There's no need to deliberately lean in or start twirling your hair madly. In some cases, if you're forcing the physical signs to show them you're interested, it can be overwhelming. Instead, just focus on making the most of your date whatever the outcome, and let your body language speak freely.

UP CLOSE & PERSONAL

ON THE DEFENSIVE
KURT & CHANTEL

Chantel, 30, has an ideal man in mind 'if you rolled them into one and covered them in sprinkles'. He's a cross between muscle-bound Khal Drogo from *Game of Thrones*, the *Fifty Shades* disciplinarian Christian Grey, and Superman alter ego Clark Kent. When she finds beefy tattoo enthusiast Kurt waiting at the bar, it really does look like she's set up with the man-sundae of her dreams. Then she discovers what he does for a living: he's a porn actor. It comes as a relief to Chantel when they both agree not to see each other again.

BODY CONFIDENCE
NICK & SIAN

Voluptuous air hostess Sian arrives at the restaurant in a figure-hugging outfit with a plunging neckline, and it's no surprise to find her date, Nick, can't keep his eyes off her. On settling in at the table, Sian happens to mention that the chair is a little tight around her 'massive podonky'. Instinctively, Nick touches his nose before assuring her that she has a nice bottom. Experts might suggest this indicates lying, but the bare fact is he's smitten by Sian, and just a little overwhelmed. The proof? Having settled down in each other's company, the couple meet up for a second date and then proceed to go blissfully steady.

SO CLOSE
PATRICK & THOMAS

When German-born Thomas, 48, meets 49-year-old dad of one, Patrick, there's no doubt he senses the spark between them might build into flames of love. Seated across the table, Thomas's eyes twinkle, while everything he shares with his blind date is accompanied by a charming smile. The couple begin to talk on a deeper level, which is when Patrick describes his ideal man as someone with kids, so they can build a 'united family'. As he listens, poor Thomas appears to deflate in his chair, and is left staring mournfully at his lap. 'I knew I couldn't really oblige with that,' as he says later on, upon which the viewing public reach out to comfort him.

BIG-NIGHT NERVES
LOUIS & ADELA

Louis is struggling to learn the language of love. 'When I meet someone I like,' admits the 25-year-old linguist plaintively, 'that's where I go wrong.' As if to put this self-assessment into practice, Adela's toes curl when Louis finds himself so overwhelmed in her presence that his cheeks turn scarlet and he stumbles in and out of sentences. He attempts to reset, looking anywhere but at his date. If only he knew that in Adela's world 'there's nothing more attractive than a gentleman', because aside from being a bag of nerves he's charming, courteous and kind. The night sees Louis landing squarely in the friend-zone, but the experience can only boost his confidence and help him to relax next time.

AND FINALLY

Of course first dates can be intimidating, but don't allow your body to show your fear. It can say so much without you actually saying a word. If you appear comfortable your date will relax more too, and the evening will flow much more smoothly if you are both happy in each other's company.

Eye contact is incredibly important when you first meet someone, and you can put someone at ease simply by smiling. Ultimately, few people can resist a nice smile.

"

Be as you wish to seem.

"

SOCRATES

Coping with Surprises

OPEN MINDS AND OPEN HEARTS

As I mentioned in Chapter 6 'Show & Tell', many people visit the restaurant who have shared a great deal. They have been brave enough to tell their dates their biggest secrets, whatever they may be, and that is an amazing thing to do. When someone opens up to you they are taking a big risk, as there's no guarantee how you'll react. There is always the fear of being rejected so you must treat these revelations in the kindest way possible.

Even if you are genuinely shocked by what they tell you, please be mindful of how they are feeling. If what they tell you is a deal breaker – maybe someone has been divorced three times and it sets off alarm bells in your head – please try to be understanding and accept that person for who and what they are. You don't know all of the circumstances, so don't be quick to judge.

If you are open-minded and empathetic it lets people know that they're OK even if they don't conform to the stereotypes we can have about relationships. Not everyone wants to be married with 2.4 children, and there are a lot of people who don't find that idea at all attractive.

Two people's ideas of love can be completely different, and that's why we must talk honestly, and talk about what love means to us. Maybe because someone else's idea of love is different from ours, we know we cannot have a relationship with them, but we can still respect their choices and ideals.

First Dates reminds us there is no such thing as normality. Everyone is an individual and it is about whatever rocks your boat. Even if two people don't fall in love they will still want the best for each other. People say we get some funny daters in the restaurant, but they are no stranger than anyone else. We all have our quirks and differences and that is what makes us unique and interesting.

> **The only way we can accept other people is by accepting ourselves.**

I don't think normality exists. Who is to say what is normal and what is not? Who makes the rules? I love diversity, and the differences between some people are what make their relationship work well. Look at when Adam and Dan came into the restaurant. Dan loves Dr Who and reads Spider-Man comics; but instead of finding that strange, Adam embraced it and allowed Dan to be who he wants to be. You should never go into a relationship hoping the other person will change.

Of course the only way we can accept other people is by accepting ourselves. I am far from perfect and I make lots of mistakes, but I try to learn and grow from each one and by doing that I understand myself better. By not judging ourselves we stop judging others.

HOW WAS IT FOR YOU?

CHARLOTTE

'My jaw just dropped, simply because it was the last thing I expected.'

Ahead of her visit to the *First Dates* restaurant, 23-year-old Leeds graduate Charlotte was picturing the kind of person she might find waiting for her at the bar. 'I just assumed it would be a guy,' she says, despite being open about a previous relationship with another woman. 'Maybe a rugby player type with a nerdy side,' she suggests. 'I figured it would be someone about my age who lived near me in the south. And then my shallow hope was that he'd have a university background,' she adds, laughing, 'simply because that's the world I'd just come from.'

Then Charlotte met Charlie, and quickly it became apparent that his degree was the only thing she could tick off her checklist. 'He's older than me, from the north, heavily pierced and tattooed,' she says. 'In the same way, Charlie was looking for a very feminine kind of girl and there I was saying how I wished I'd come to the restaurant in my trackies! We got along just fine right from the start – and I'm sure a rugby-playing geek would've turned out to be a complete melon – but I couldn't help wondering what else there was about Charlie and me that made us a potential match. Then again, I kicked off our date with a couple of drinks, so I didn't give it too much thought.'

Having settled at their table and begun talking about their lives, Charlie mentioned an ex. As Charlotte had already told him about her bisexuality, she immediately wondered if Charlie might've been involved with another man. 'I thought, "That's it. He's gay but interested in dating a woman."'

While Charlotte was all ears, and kept her cool when Charlie confirmed he dated women, nothing could've prepared her for his revelation that he had in fact been born a girl. 'My jaw just dropped, simply because it was the last thing I expected,' she says. 'I had absolutely no idea.' At the same time, when she found her voice once more Charlotte's response demonstrated why the pair were destined to get along so well. 'It took a moment for me to get over the shock,' she says. 'After that, I just wanted to make sure whatever I said next showed respect. Charlie must've been terrified of my reaction before he spoke up. As it honestly made no difference to me I simply told him that I didn't care. I was speaking from the heart, even though my mind was reeling in surprise.'

Charlotte is naturally open-minded, a quality that comes into its own on a blind date. 'When you're learning about someone new it's crucial that you don't judge,' she says. 'Even if they tell you something deeply personal about themself, you still don't know that much about them. It just makes it all part of the discovery process, and shows that person feels comfortable enough in your company to share intimate information, which is flattering. I suppose some people in my position might've reacted badly, and even got up and left, but that would've said more about them than Charlie.'

> **❛ It took a moment for me to get over the shock. ❜**

For many people in Charlotte's situation, a bombshell of this nature would steer the conversation. But instead of pushing Charlie for details of his journey, Charlotte's sole focus lay in what made him tick. 'I was interested in him and his outlook on life, not this one experience he'd been through. I also thought that had I fixated on the surgical aspect that would've defined me through his eyes, and possibly been an uncomfortable subject. I just wanted to use the opportunity to get to know him better.'

Having been in the hot seat when a date springs a surprise, does Charlotte have advice for anyone who feels the need to share something significant with a relative stranger? 'It's your decision,' she says. 'You do have to be prepared to answer any questions, and that's totally fair enough if your date's trying to understand things, but it's down to you to decide when the time feels right. It might be soon after you've met, just to get it off your chest, or at a later date when you feel more comfortable in their company. There are no rules. What matters is that you both relate to each other with respect.'

While Charlotte and Charlie gave a masterclass in managing a surprise on a first date, how did the couple fare on leaving the restaurant? 'We went for drinks afterwards, and that was lovely,' she says. 'With everything out in the open, it meant we just chatted and enjoyed what was left of the evening with no sense that one of us was holding anything back. When Charlie told me about himself he'd been quite reserved,' she adds. 'I'm sure that was down to the fact that he wasn't sure how I'd react, but once we'd built up some trust he shone.'

Even though Charlie's situation hadn't fazed Charlotte one little bit, and even served as a bonding moment, she feels the spark between them was always going to settle into something platonic. 'We live far apart from one another, and I'd just started a new job that means I'm in London every other week,' she explains. 'What's more, soon after our date Charlie underwent surgery, and so he needed time to focus on himself. But we talk on a regular basis, and I really value his friendship. Looking back, it was a great date because we both felt comfortable. If you're relaxed then you can be open about any issue, and that's when you really get to know each other.'

SAM SAYS

If you ever have to deal with a curve ball on a date, try and handle it with empathy and a smile. You should never judge anybody, no matter how much of a bombshell it is.

If someone tells you something that catches you by surprise you should always take time to process it before you react. Just imagine how hard it must have been for your date to open up to you. Even if what they tell you freaks you out a bit, be respectful. Charlie's secret was a big one, and he dealt with telling Charlotte incredibly well. I also think Charlotte handled it brilliantly, because it must have come as a shock. She's clearly open-minded, and she knew that the fact Charlie was born a girl didn't define him because there was so much more to him.

Charlie's honesty kicked off an interesting conversation and enabled him and Charlotte to get to know each other quickly. The trust was there straight away, and neither of them held back.

Everyone has a past and everyone has secrets. Your date isn't meeting you so they can give you a stamp of approval for being perfect. Perfection is not real, and if someone doesn't like the way you are or what you tell them about yourself, they're obviously not right for you.

> ❛ *Everyone has a past and everyone has secrets.* ❜

If I was ever on a date with someone who told me they were transgender I would be interested in their life; I would feel privileged that they'd shared something so personal with me. I would respect them for having the confidence to walk into a situation and be so open where someone could easily judge them.

If you tell someone something you're scared about admitting and they accept it you're on to a winner. If you have a secret that could potentially make or break a relationship I do think it's important to be upfront. But only if you're comfortable with it. There's no rule that says you have to tell anyone anything until you're ready.

Dating is all about being respectful to others. I've been on dates where I've realized it is not going anywhere, but I will still listen to whatever the other person has got to say and enjoy their story. I always try to find something interesting in every situation.

It never hurts to spend an evening with someone whose company you enjoy, even if you know they're not going to be the love of your life. Take what you can from every situation and sprinkle a little bit of sunshine on it.

UP CLOSE & PERSONAL

BARING THE TRUTH
WARREN & ROCHELLE

Adult TV presenter Rochelle has revealed her profession to motivational speaker Warren. He's a little shocked, but Rochelle is ready. 'I'm just a woman,' she reasons. 'I'm confident and I can play with my sexuality.' Warren does his best to be cool, but it's clear this revelation has derailed his date expectations. 'I couldn't imagine other guys looking at my girlfriend's bosoms,' he admits later, even though Rochelle is not a woman to be defined by her work and potentially made the perfect match. In a bid to salvage something from the evening, he suggests meeting again 'as brother and sister', which is met by disbelief from Rochelle and not a little laughter from them both.

DEATH BY CANDLELIGHT
CHRIS & ZINA

Having settled in at the table, the couple are just finding their way into a conversation. Working in the funeral trade, Chris feels he has to get his profession into the open sooner rather than later. It's just a question of finding a good time to break it gently to Zina so she isn't lost for words. 'So, what do you do?' she asks with a lovely warm smile. 'I handle stiffs,' Chris replies in a way that effectively stops time around the table. 'Okaaaay,' says Zina after a moment, in a masterclass of recovery and poise.

THE NUMBERS GAME
SCOTT & VICTORIA

'So, now I know how this is going to be,' says smitten sales manager Scott, when Victoria reveals how OCD affects her life. With a thing for the numbers 2, 5, 7 and 9, Victoria knows she'll struggle if his numbers don't add up.

'What date's your birthday?' she asks. Hesitantly, Scott informs her it's the 16th, and Victoria punches the air. 'That's good because six and one is seven!' Scott takes a moment to get his head around the figures, but as the date progresses it's clear this makes Victoria all the more endearing to him. Fast-forward to a Christmas celebration at the restaurant, where Scott proposes on one knee, and then rises to his feet as if he's just won the Lottery.

THE WOMAN IN ME
BEN & CHLOE

'Are we putting it all out on the table?' asks Ben, 21, having admitted a penchant for One Direction. Chloe, 22, invites him to open right up. 'We've gone quite far already,' she points out. So Ben takes a deep breath and reveals all. 'I occasionally cross-dress,' he announces. The couple have barely met, but it's clear that Ben feels relaxed enough in her company to share his innermost secret, and Chloe rises magnificently to the occasion. Afterwards, she admits to being taken aback, but flattered that Ben had felt comfortable enough to be so open. The result? The promise of a follow-up date.

❧ AND FINALLY ❧

Life is not a smooth, straight road and there will be surprises along the way. Some will be good and some will be bad, but they will all be character-building in some way.

Believing in yourself, self-love and understanding underpin everything. Once you truly love who you are, you can truly love others. Accept yourself, and you can accept those around you. Be kind and good and always treat people how you wish people to treat you.

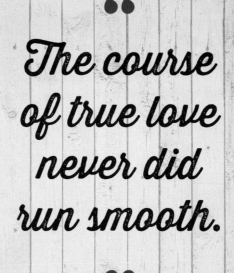

"

The course
of true love
never did
run smooth.

"

WILLIAM SHAKESPEARE
A MIDSUMMER NIGHT'S DREAM

Drinking & Dating

♥

Chapter Nine

LOVE AND INTOXICATION

Having a drink before a date can help you feel a bit more relaxed and lower your inhibitions. But it does become a problem when people drink too much and go over the top.

You need to know your limits because you don't want to become incoherent. Drinking will probably make you feel less shy in the beginning, but it can get embarrassing and you may end up sending out the wrong message.

When people get to the point where they have to be escorted out of the restaurant or asked to stop drinking – which has happened a few times – it doesn't give a great impression to someone you want to see again. It could put someone off if you're too drunk and it could mean you don't get another date. Personally it would put me off. But I can't speak for other people.

It also depends how alcohol affects you. Some people can have several drinks and be fine, whereas others may act a bit silly, which can be annoying if the other person is abstaining. If both people on the date are drinking it is easier in a way, but if only one person is drinking they can be on two totally different levels.

> **❛ Don't be that person who gets completely hammered when their date is sipping sparkling water. ❜**

I've been working in restaurants for twenty-five years and if there's one thing I cannot bear it is talking to people who are ridiculously drunk. There are some people who are still 'sober' when they're drunk and they can make a lot of sense. And then there are people who completely lose the plot. It is awful when people talk nonsense and think they're being incredibly interesting, when actually they've told the same story three times.

Some people turn up to the restaurant very drunk and I never think that's a good idea because then their date is not meeting the real them. They're meeting a drunk and probably more confident version. And how is someone supposed to get to know who you actually are?

I would say that it is fine to have a few drinks on a first date, but drink in moderation. If you and your date end up going on to a bar after dinner and getting drunk that is not a bad thing because it is nice to get drunk together. It is a fun thing to share. But please don't be that person who gets completely hammered when their date is sipping sparkling water. That is never going to end well.

HOW WAS IT FOR YOU?

ANNA

'Looking back, I should have eaten because that would have sobered me up a bit.'

A bit of social lubrication is standard before a blind date, but legal secretary Anna was so nervous about her dinner she may have gone over the top when building up Dutch courage. 'I'd been out and bought a new outfit that day but I still felt unprepared. I spent ages getting my make-up perfect, and because I was going on a dinner date I didn't eat beforehand. I had a glass of wine at home to take the edge off my nerves and that turned into a bottle. Wine gets me drunk pretty quickly anyway, and it was even worse on an empty stomach.'

Anna had a couple of gins on the way to the restaurant, and another glass of white wine while she was waiting to make her grand entrance. Despite the liquid confidence she still felt terrified as she prepared to meet her date. 'I walked into the restaurant and Fred said, "Don't be nervous." That's when I thought, "What am I doing here? Can I go home please?" I was scared. I'd been on a couple of Tinder dates the year before but that doesn't feel like a first date in a way. You know what someone looks like and you've already chatted to them a bit. Simon was already sat at the bar when I arrived so I said hello and ordered a vodka and cranberry. That's when I realized I was a bit drunk.'

Anna thought it was best to come clean to Simon and admit she'd already sunk a few beforehand – especially as the last thing she wanted to do at that point was sit down for a big meal. 'I told Simon I was half cut. Looking back, I should have eaten because that would have sobered me up a bit. Simon suggested we had a couple of tequilas and because I was already on my way I was happy to carry on. He seemed up for it too, so I thought, "Why not?"'

The pair carried on drinking and chatting and then, buoyed up by a few more drinks, Anna let exactly what was in her head come out of her mouth. 'I told Simon he looked like a black Phil Mitchell, which he wasn't too happy about. But he did! I also asked him a lot of questions about his tattoos and family, but he didn't ask me any questions so I thought he wasn't interested. It wasn't like I fancied him either and we just didn't click. We're very different.'

With the date dead in the water Anna decided to make the most of the evening, which involved her hosting a disco for one in the bar area. 'I felt like the whole thing had gone out the window so I started messing around and dancing. I was just having a laugh. I wanted to make the best of a bad situation. I know it looked like I was the drunk one but Simon was egging me on to drink and he was the one ordering shots. He was a decent guy but even if we'd really fancied each other it would never have worked.'

Instead of letting her initial *First Dates* experience put her off, the 29-year-old came back for round two with stripper Junior. 'Junior wasn't for me at all, but he was a nice guy and we got on OK. He said he had to rush off after the date to get to Birmingham to do some naked butlering, so we were never going to make a night of it. We did actually manage to eat dinner that time but it wasn't romantic. I had a few drinks but not as many as I'd had on the first date. Maybe if I had it would have been more fun.'

> ❛ *He seemed up for it too, so I thought, "Why not?"* ❜

Would Anna recommend others drink before meeting a potential partner? 'If you're drinking beforehand because you're nervous you shouldn't go on the date and put yourself through that torture. Dates should be enjoyable. The only reason I drank on the dates with Simon and Junior was because it was going to be on telly and I was petrified about what people would think of me.

I probably made things worse overall. It's fine to have a drink before a date and then another couple during, but it's not a great idea to get hammered.'

Anna is single and on the lookout at the moment, and says her days of drinking a bottle of wine and several gins before a date are over. 'I am going out on dates but I've deleted Tinder because I've decided to leave it up to fate and try and

meet someone the traditional way. I hope I meet someone, and I have to say that since the show a lot more people come up to me so it's a good way of meeting people generally. I do feel like I've grown up a bit since I was on *First Dates* and if I went on a date with someone I liked now I would try and behave myself. It's great to have a laugh, but it's nice to show someone the real you first meet. And that's got to be the vaguely sober you.'

LAURA SAYS

When couples order a bottle of wine to go with their meal at the restaurant, I know the date is going alright. It's something they can share and enjoy together at the same pace. To be honest, issues only really kick in if one of you is miles ahead of the other.

First impressions can last a long time when you're meeting as strangers. You don't have anything else to go on except how that person presents themself, so if they've had a few in advance it's hard to ignore. They might be fun company, as Simon discovered with Anna on her first visit, but it's spoiling the chance for you to find out what they're really like. What's more, drink doesn't make everyone want to laugh, joke and dance around the tables. If someone saw me drunk on a first date, I can guarantee things wouldn't work out. I am not on best form. I don't even know what I'm saying most of the time.

It's understandable why people might turn to alcohol to see them through a blind date. It can boost your confidence, but then it's totally natural to be nervous when you meet someone in an intimate environment like a restaurant. I'd even say it's flattering if you arrive with butterflies because it shows the date is important to you. Rocking up tipsy or drunk might cover those insecurities, but I see no reason to hide how you're really feeling. If my date admitted he was nervous I'd think it was sweet, and probably be a little relieved as no doubt I'd be feeling the same way. That's the moment when you can suggest a drink together. It can help you to ease into what might be a challenging but hopefully fun social situation.

Everyone is different, of course. Some people don't drink at all, and good on them. I can't say I'd make it through without a glass, but when it comes to any kind of alcohol you do have to know your limits. So, even if you feel the need for a little Dutch courage ahead of your date, or while waiting at the bar if you're first to arrive, you need to ask yourself if you're going to be able to handle any more if that person suggests a drink. You don't want to be saying you've already had enough. Sharing a glass or two is a moment to savour as a couple, which is why I'd always recommend arriving sober. It might take guts, but it gives you more leeway so that drinking doesn't come between you and the chances of spending more time together.

> *It's totally natural to be nervous when you meet someone . . . it's flattering if you arrive with butterflies because it shows the date is important to you.*

If things work out, and you see each other again, then there could well be a time and place when you really hit the booze in their company. That's completely different than getting drunk on a first date. Why? Because as wild as you might become they know what you're like sober, and that should be the person they fell for in the first place.

UP CLOSE & PERSONAL

THE WAY HE TELLS 'EM
AARON & DARCY

'Is that a mirror in your pants?' asks part-time funny man, and full-time TV aerial erector, Aaron. 'Because I can see myself in them.' Fortunately for nursery worker Darcy, her date gets this one out of his system before they actually meet, but that doesn't stop him from bringing his one-liners and double entendres to the bar. On kicking off proceedings by ordering two Jägerbombs, Aaron downs his in one and then inquires if Darcy is 'good at swallowing'. Watching her set down her empty glass with a grimace, barman Merlin looks entirely prepared for her to order several more to see her through the evening.

PINTS OF CONFIDENCE
RYAN & HELEN

'I want to punch above my weight,' jokes Ryan, 33, recently single after a long-term relationship. With such high expectations, it's no surprise that he's nervous. So what better way to steady the ship than a whacking great pint at the bar? When stunning Helen, 29, makes her appearance, Ryan reaches for his drink once more. With Dutch courage in full effect, he's more than ready to greet her when she hops on to her stool. 'Are you nervous?' he asks. 'I'm not at all!' While the date proves spirited – washed down with a bottle of wine – it doesn't end in love. Or even a hug. Refreshed Ryan spreads his hands, but Helen counters with the offer of a sobering handshake.

DRINKING FOR TWO
DANNY & LAUREN

'I'm looking for someone more polite than arrogant,' says hairdresser Lauren, 29. Essex boy Danny, 38, certainly fits the bill in theory. He's polite, far from arrogant, but also set to get a teeny bit plastered. 'A pint and a Jägerbomb, please,' he requests ahead of their meal. 'Actually, make that two Jägerbombs, and if she doesn't want it, I'll have it.' Lauren might be taken aback by her date's boozy enthusiasm, and though it doesn't end in love she freely admits he's been very good company. 'I'd set you up with my friend,' she offers at the end, and we can only hope it's someone who can match Danny drink for drink.

CHAMPAGNE FOR THE LADY
TOM & ALLIEE

Suave Tom is a 'big house, nice wife and some fast cars' kind of guy, and tonight he's taking steps to strike one off the list. Arriving early, with flowers in hand for his blind date, he asks Fred to line up champagne for their table. Some roses and a bottle of bubbly is the quickest way to a girl's heart, right? As he discovers, when Alliee walks straight into a date to find the romance level dialled up to eleven, it all proves a bit too much. After talking it over on the phone with a mate, she returns with a winning smile and gives Tom the chance to simply be himself. Which he does, by dropping the fizz for good conversation, and earns himself a second date.

✦ AND FINALLY ✦

Should you have a few drinks on a date? Why not?
Should you have shots at the bar before you've even
sat down to dinner? No.

Drink to enjoy yourself and enhance the evening,
not to get drunk. We are never as funny and clever
as we think we are after too much wine. The drunk
you is not the real you, and the real you is who your
date wants to get to know. Alcohol should be a nice
addition to a date, but not the focus.

"

Never go to excess,
but let moderation
be your guide.

"

CICERO

SAM

FROM:

London

BEST DATE EVER:

At a rave in Cornwall a few years ago. We went with other people as a group and it was so much fun. It was no holds barred and we were able to relax and have a laugh without any pressure.

WORST DATE EVER:

It was when I was at uni. It was the classic 'dinner and drinks' date but it was a bit of a disaster because I still liked a girl I'd just broken up with. Never go on a date with a new person until you're over someone else.

FIRST KISS:

At my Year 7 disco, with a girl called Rose. We danced with our arms out straight, so I was a total gentleman.

CRUSH:

Holly Willoughby. She seems good fun.

PERFECT ROMANTIC NIGHT OUT:

It would be a big warehouse with a lovely sound system, amazing door staff and great people. I know that doesn't sound that romantic but there's nothing wrong with dates that are a bit different.

PERFECT ROMANTIC NIGHT IN:

A perfect night in starts with meeting in a nice pub for a game of pool, and then heading back home to watch a nice film with wine and nibbles. And maybe some cheese if you're really going for it.

GO-TO DATE OUTFIT:

A nice fitted shirt, skinny jeans and some decent, clean trainers. I'm a big fan of socks, so I build my outfit around them and make sure everything is coordinated.

EVER HAD A MISHAP AT THE RESTAURANT?

I've never dropped food on anyone – I'm a professional – but I have occasionally spilled a small bit of wine on a tablecloth here and there.

FAVOURITE *FIRST DATES* COUPLE:

Adam and Dan. They seem so happy together.

> ❝ Unless you throw yourself into it, you just don't know if something is going to work. ❞

FUNNIEST *FIRST DATES* MOMENT:

Every night is funny working with the people I do. They're amazing.

WHAT HAS WORKING ON *FIRST DATES* TAUGHT YOU ABOUT LOVE?

Unless you throw yourself into it, you just don't know if something is going to work. I've been out with people where it should have worked and it didn't, but I've never regretted giving it a go.

WHY SHOULD PEOPLE GO ON *FIRST DATES*?

Because love is timeless, free and never-ending. Nobody should ever stop looking for love. *First Dates* is an honest representation of how people can find people. Love truly blossoms.

Time Out

Chapter Ten

A DATE OF TWO HALVES

A lot of people who come into the restaurant will go to the bathroom at some point to phone someone or take a moment to themselves.

I personally don't think it is a great idea to take a break in the middle of a date and gossip in the toilets or ask for advice. You've got to be able to stand on your own two feet and you can't phone your mum every five minutes. You need to be independent and make up your own mind.

Having said that, if phoning someone will relax you and help you to enjoy the date more it is not doing any harm, and it seems to work for a lot of people. Phoning a friend or relative gives some people more courage, or a sense that they are not alone.

Sometimes a dater simply wants to phone someone to say, 'Oh, I've met this incredible guy or girl,' and that can be very nice. Sometimes you want to share your joy as soon as you can, and it can be a release for the excitement you feel so you can be a bit cooler when you return to the table.

The hope is always that someone is having such a good time on their date they won't want to take that time out. If the date is wonderful you should want to spend as much time as possible with the other person.

Some people will go outside to have a cigarette several times during a romantic meal. That may be the time when they take a step back and reflect on everything, but if you're only on a date for two hours why would you want to waste so much time?

If you need to analyse everything when you're with someone you may be thinking a little too much, or you are not on the right date. You assess how it is going as you go along and know instinctively if there is something between you. Remember too much analysis is paralysis in the end. So just live and let live, and enjoy the moment.

It is like going to a restaurant for the first time. You can discuss the food and the staff and the location for hours, but the bottom line is: Would you go back? Dates work in the same way. You could analyse it for hours but the only question you need to be asking yourself is whether or not you would like to see that person again. If you have to overthink it, and try and convince yourself you do, the chances are you don't.

> ❛ *If you need to analyse everything when you're with someone you may be thinking a little too much, or you are not on the right date.* ❜

HOW WAS IT FOR YOU?

MARIA

'It's a chance to put my thoughts into words and hear them back.'

'My confidence took a knock when I split up with my long-term partner,' says Maria, 44. 'You go through a sense of bereavement, but I've learned a lot about myself since then. Eventually, I thought I can either stay indoors or get out there again and see what happens.'

For anyone who finds themself single once again, jumping back into the dating scene takes confidence. It's natural to need a little encouragement or hand-holding. In Maria's case her arrival at the restaurant was made all the more memorable by the fact that she brought her 24-year-old daughter, Charlotte, to meet a blind date of her own. Talk to this warm and instantly likeable mother from Newbury, however, and it quickly becomes clear who was in the supportive role. 'Charlotte can get really nervous before a date,' she says. 'I often see her looking wobbly, thinking she can't go through with it, while I tend to be more excited at the prospect of going out. Of course, I was just as nervous when we waited at the bar, but I definitely felt like a mother as well as a dater.'

Maria jokes that her ideal man would be in his sixties with a dodgy heart and lots of money, but in reality she arrived hoping that Cupid would look kindly upon her. That moment before a date walks through the door can weigh heavily, and it was helpful to be able to focus on Charlotte as a means of distraction. Maria is also keenly aware that when her man did show up he might not expect to find her daughter in tow. 'Steve introduced himself and immediately asked, "What's going on here, then?" I had to explain that we don't normally go on dates together, but it definitely caught him off guard. After that, Fred showed us to our table and Charlotte was free to meet her date, Ben, on her own.'

Despite dining on opposite sides of the restaurant, both mother and daughter quickly established a line of communication. 'I could see her over Steve's shoulder,' Maria chuckles. 'It was clear she was thrilled by Ben and his big biceps because she gestured with her arm. But I really needed to focus on Steve, and so I asked him to move to one side to shield me from her. In response, Charlotte just leaned the other way, so there was no escape.'

Watching this double date unfold, it was evident that Maria and Charlotte are incredibly close. 'Steve had excused himself to use the loo,' she explains. 'Sitting on my own, I couldn't resist signalling to Charlotte to get her attention. As soon as she saw me, I started pointing towards the Ladies. To my horror, she just spelled it out to Ben, who gave her full permission for us to "go and have a powwow".'

Maria believes she knows her daughter well, and so it was no surprise when Charlotte met her in front of the mirror and voiced enthusiasm for Ben. 'She likes the big guys,' laughs Maria, 'and that's what she got. Straight away she was saying, "Oh my God, Mum, he's gorgeous. Isn't he lush?" She was basically looking for validation, which everyone wants when they've met someone new that they like. She was too excited to ask me much about Steve,' she points out, 'but by then I'd already worked out that he was a really nice guy.' And did Maria have any advice for her daughter before they returned to the table? 'I just told her to calm it down on the drink if she really liked him,' she laughs.

For many daters the half-time break has become a familiar fixture. You've just been through an intense experience, after all. Having met a stranger, and focused on getting to know each other, those few minutes apart can serve several purposes. It isn't for everyone, but it certainly works for some, as Maria agrees. 'I've often been straight on the phone to Charlotte or a friend,' she admits. 'Especially if I'm at all unsure about my date. Sometimes I don't even need their advice. It's just a chance to put my thoughts into words and hear them back. Then there's the opportunity to check yourself in the mirror and brush your hair. It all helps as a kind of reality check, a way to get things in perspective, and means you go back feeling refreshed and properly grounded.'

As Maria and many other daters will testify, time out from any first date is always useful, whether it's a cry for help – leading to a well-timed text message calling you home – or a chance to get a grip because you've met 'the One'. But how does it feel when it's your turn to be left waiting at the table? 'I'm good at working out how they're feeling before they take a break,' says Maria with a smile. 'Nobody has tried to climb out through the window on me yet.'

Maria considers the unusual one-off arrangement a success. 'Steve is such a great guy,' she says. 'We talked so much throughout the rest of the date, and went out again several times afterwards. Unfortunately we live some distance from each other and so things never went further. I still consider him to be a friend,' she adds, 'and we're in touch regularly.' As for Charlotte and her man of many muscles? Maria explains that although the same geographical factor came between her and Ben, she also looks back on their evening in the *First Dates* restaurant with happy memories. 'We both needed that nudge to give it a go,' she says, 'and ended up sharing a great experience.'

> ❛ *I'm good at working out how they're feeling before they take a break . . . Nobody has tried to climb out through the window on me yet.* ❜

SAM SAYS

The whole 'time out' thing is quite strange. On the one hand, I do understand why people do it because they're often nervous or they want some space to mull things over. But on the other hand, if a date is going well the last thing you want to do is spend ages on the phone to one of your mates analysing it; you want to be with the other person having a brilliant time.

I can see why Charlotte and Maria took time out during their date. They were both in the restaurant at the same time and they must have been desperate to talk things over. But it must have been uncomfortable for their dates to know that they were being discussed in the toilets; it would have made me feel self-conscious knowing someone was discussing me while I was sat at a table on my own. If you're feeling panicked and the only way you can get through a date is by talking to someone who pulls you back down to earth, fair enough. I've never done it but if it's what's going to get you

through, it's up to you. If a conversation with someone you're close to is going to make your night more enjoyable then go for it. Just don't stay in the toilet all night. A date for one isn't a lot of fun.

Girls probably take time out more than guys because girls want to talk to their mates about that kind of thing more. I can't imagine one of my mates phoning me from a date to tell me how it's going. It would be very weird.

I'm old school, so I think taking time out on a date for any reason isn't the done thing. I'd feel bad if I left someone hanging. I don't even like people having a phone on the table during a date because it shows you're not engaged with the conversation.

If someone got their phone out and started using it at the table during dinner it would be a massive turn-off for me because a date should have your full attention.

I'm aware of other people's mannerisms on dates; body language says so much, and you can't read signs if you're looking at your phone or itching to call your mum. Your focus should be on the person in front of you. You shouldn't be thinking, 'I can't wait to tell my best mate what kind of shirt he's got on.'

❛ *Don't stay in the toilet all night.*
A date for one isn't a lot of fun. ❜

UP CLOSE & PERSONAL

EYES ON THE PRIZE
KENNY & JESS

Smooth-talking beauty salon owner Kenny knows how to charm a lady. He certainly can't help but switch into velvet-tongued mode for his date, Jess. Her figure-hugging dress becomes a topic of conversation,

because poor Kenny freely admits that it's doing strange things to him. In need of a break from the heat billowing from Kenny's side of the table, Jess excuses herself for a moment in the loo and a chance to reflect on things over the phone with her mate. Meantime, Kenny's eye turns to a lone female diner at a table nearby. She manages to resist his charms, but Jess returns with her eyes wide open. 'My bullshit detector is on red alert,' she tells us later.

A BREAK TO REMEMBER
DAVID & ALEX

Anaesthetist David, 28, is used to rendering people senseless, but only marketing manager Alex, 26, can account for his sudden memory lapse. 'I've forgotten your name,' he confesses, midway through a meal that saw the couple bonding over chat about gay rugby. David

stops with his 'Lady Diana eyes', and chooses instead to make his date sweat. 'I'm going to the bathroom and you can think about it,' he says after several torturous minutes, but the break makes no difference to Alex. 'Please tell me,' he begs David on his return, and suggests in desperation that this prematurely senior moment has a medical cause. 'It's a condition!'

SCORE
MOUSTAFA & MEGAN

In a moment of misjudgement, or sheer madness, oil executive Moustafa decides to rate his date, Megan, a six out of ten for her appearance. Our lovely Yorkshire lass laughs it off, despite pointing out that in his view it means she's only just scraped past the halfway mark. Then Moustafa awards himself an eight, and immediately Megan excuses herself for a smoke outside. There, on the phone to a mate, she gets it out of her system before returning to endure the second half. 'He's just a massive douche,' she says, before crushing the cigarette stub under her stiletto.

LONG CALL
MUHALA & FRANKIE

'What is he doing?' mutters Frankie, several minutes after her date, Muhala, pops to the Gents. As it turns out, Muhala is on the phone to a confidante, reviewing what has been one sexually charged meeting of body and mind. 'She's hot,' he confirms, pacing manfully in front of the mirror, only to register that time is also ticking. 'I can't be in here for too long,' he says with a note of panic. 'I don't want her thinking I'm going for a shit.' With the call closed, Muhala is through the door in a mad scramble and confidently back in the game.

❧ AND FINALLY ☙

If you feel like you want time away from your date, I must be honest, that is not a great sign. Of course, you might have an urge to tell someone else how wonderful they are, but in my view that can wait. You should feel like you want to spend as much time with them as possible, and even be arranging the second date in your head.

In many ways, a date is like a piece of music. It should carry you both along and feel rich in emotion. Taking a break can interrupt that flow, but if you must take a moment in the restroom, make it quick and be sure to bring even more energy and charm to the table when you return.

"

Absence makes the heart grow fonder.

"

ANON.

Sexual Chemistry

Chapter Eleven

THAT CERTAIN SOMETHING

When I think of chemistry between the daters who have visited the restaurant I always think back to Frankie and Muhala. There was passion there from the start and they couldn't take their eyes off each other. That kind of connection is unmistakable. You could feel and see it.

They were both good-looking and both dancers, which gave them a lot to talk about straight away. But more than that, they had a fire between them. I remember thinking, 'When they leave after this date, they're going to have more than a drink . . .'

Sexual chemistry is either there or it is not. It is not often something you can create, but it can become more apparent the better you get to know someone. Humour or intelligence can be a huge turn-on, and a spark can be ignited if someone makes you laugh or interests you greatly. A person's mind can be a very sexy thing. And the more you like someone in general, the more attracted to them you can be, and the better the sex becomes.

You don't always have real sexual compatibility with whoever you're with, but sex is always nice because you're in that special place and it is intimate. Even if it is not always as good as it could be, you can still have a great time. Sex moves to a different level when it feels like there are fireworks going off as soon as you meet each other.

On the downside you do have to wonder how long you can keep that momentum going. What if sexual chemistry is the only thing that's holding your relationship together and then it fades away? What are you left with? Very little, sadly.

Sexual chemistry is incredible but you don't always have it with someone who is right for you. At times you can have it with someone you may not even like that much, but you have such a strong attraction you decide to have a good time for a little while. As long as you are both on the same page and open about how you feel, that can be a wonderful thing.

> *Sex moves to a different level when it feels like there are fireworks going off as soon as you meet each other.*

Sex with someone you don't know very well can be exciting. It is not always easy for people to be completely uninhibited about what they like when they're in a relationship with someone they care deeply for. Sometimes when you have a few dates with someone knowing it won't go any further you feel free and can be more candid.

Some people have inhibitions and some people are open to anything. If you and a partner are not compatible and you both like very different things it can make a relationship hard and it can cause problems. For that reason it is something you should talk about early on in your relationship. But not too early. I would never start talking about sex to someone on a first date – unless I either had an instant bond with them, or we knew we just wanted to have a good time and nothing else. Sex is an amazing thing and the most important thing is that you both feel comfortable discussing it. So if you need to wait, wait. There's no rush. Sex should always be mutual and respectful. And a lot of fun.

HOW WAS IT FOR YOU?

FRANKIE

'We were basically having sex with each other's eyes.'

Sometimes a couple just click, and when Frankie and Muhala first met the spark was so obvious it was Bonfire Night and New Year's Eve rolled into one. 'The minute Muhala walked into the restaurant I knew he was my date and I was so happy,' says Frankie. 'He's absolutely beautiful and so my type. There was a connection between us straight away. I looked into his eyes and I could tell that we were both like, "Oh, HELLO!" Before we'd even spoken we both knew what was happening. Or rather, what was going to happen.'

The pair were soon flirting over a plate of olives, and when they sat down to dinner 22-year-old Frankie admits it was hard to keep her mind on the food. 'We were talking for ages but we were basically having sex with each other's eyes while we were doing it. We're both dancers and we had loads of other things in common, but underlying every conversation was this sexual tension. It wasn't like we talked about sex loads or anything, but we were so attracted to each other it didn't need to be said.'

Much like Frankie's comment about her unusual allergy, which caused raised eyebrows all round. 'My problem is that I've got no filter and I come out with whatever is in my head. Muhala and I were chatting away and I blurted out that I was allergic to latex. I immediately regretted it because I didn't mean anything by it. It's one of those things I need to stop telling people because I always get a weird reaction. You need to keep that kind of thing to yourself.

It didn't make things awkward in any way, though, and after a few drinks we both knew where that night was heading. We were both single, we fancied each other, and without either of us having to actually say the words we knew we were going to make a night of it.'

And, indeed, a morning. The pair stayed out drinking until 4 a.m. before heading back to Muhala's house. 'We went to a bar in Covent Garden and we talked for hours and hours. We got quite giddy and silly and we ended up taking a spontaneous train to Brighton where Muhala lives. We went out for breakfast the following day and I met some of his friends. We went on the pier and messed about and we had a great time. He's a lovely guy.'

Frankie and Muhala carried on seeing each other as and when they could, but the fact that Muhala works nights and Frankie works days meant eventually things fizzled out. 'We had a great time together and we still talk and text a lot now. Whenever we see each other that chemistry is still totally there. It just never goes away. If the situation was different and we weren't both so busy something would have properly kicked off between us. We really liked each other and it wasn't all about the sex at all. We definitely had a sexual connection but we also enjoyed spending time with each other . . . we didn't spend the whole time in bed.'

While Frankie believes it is very important, she doesn't think that sexual chemistry alone can keep you and a partner together long term. 'You can't build a relationship just on sex, because if that's all you've got it's not going to last. Because you can have amazing sexual chemistry with someone but not actually like them that much. I don't think you can create sexual chemistry either. You either have it or you don't. I've got so many male friends I've known for years and they're fit guys, but nothing's ever happened between us because we don't have that connection. Sometimes two people will lock eyes and they know straight away that they want to take each other to bed.'

Does Frankie think that having sexual chemistry makes a date more exciting or more nerve-racking? 'It can be a bit of both but it's definitely more exciting at first – your stomach flips over. The feeling is amazing. It's all about the way someone looks at you, and the butterflies. However, I do seem to attract the sort who have only got one thing on their minds, which can be frustrating.

> **The feeling is amazing. It's all about the way someone looks at you, and the butterflies.**

Maybe I'm putting out the wrong vibes? Sometimes there's no rhyme or reason for who you have chemistry with. You can meet a guy who's absolutely gorgeous and you feel like you should fancy him, but you don't feel anything. And you may get introduced to someone you find hugely attractive, but if the guy's a total idiot that can completely ruin things. I could meet the best-looking guy in the world but if he's not very nice I'll stop fancying him – chemistry or not.'

Frankie is on the lookout for her Mr Right, and she's keeping an open mind. 'I don't have any specific requirements. When you meet someone you just know. Whether that's because you get on well or because you have chemistry, it just kind of happens. Ideally you'll have both. That's the dream.'

CICI SAYS

Frankie and Muhala are my favourite couple ever. Why? Because it was so ridiculously obvious that they fancied each other. When Muhala walked in, Frankie took one look at him and practically purred with pleasure. Moments later, he sneaked a glimpse at her bum. The grin on his face spoke volumes.

The thing about Frankie is that she's one sexy woman. Seriously, she's gorgeous. She has this body that boys can't stop looking at. What's so brilliant is that she carries herself in a way that tells them that they're going to have to work to earn her attention. Very quickly, Muhala made it clear that he was interested, and prepared to put in the effort. His body language was all about her, and she responded to him in the same way. Within minutes, it was on – and they hadn't even reached their table.

Usually, when couples on a blind date fancy each other they still go through a kind of courtship stage. There's lots of flirting, of course, but also a great deal of conversation. With Frankie and Muhala, it was just so physical. They were leaning in and offering each other olives on sticks at the earliest opportunity.

I have to say that waitressing their table was an experience that evening. Even when a couple are really into each other, they always censor themselves when I'm serving. I only have to approach and they'll pull back, change the subject perhaps, and default to best behaviour. Frankie and Muhala were having far too much of a hot time to break for me. They were ever so polite, but the whole provocative talk and double entendre thing between them didn't stop. Put it this way, I never once heard them chatting about families; it was animal attraction from start to finish. The fact that they were both dancers made it all the more exciting. That gave them something in common, but also made it clear that they were both in touch with their bodies. I think we all knew where this date was heading when they climbed into a taxi.

Back in the restaurant, Frankie and Muhala's visit left us with one question on our minds. To what extent is physical attraction enough to make a good date? We agreed it was totally fine if you both know where it's going, as this couple clearly did. If you share the view that it's enough, and you're both happy with that, then why not? But difficulties can creep in if one of you is hoping for something more. It boils down to being entirely upfront with each other.

Otherwise one of you risks being hurt if you both get swept up in the moment and there's nothing on the other side. If there's any doubt in your mind, it's so important that you're always able to say something like, 'Listen, I really fancy you, but I'm looking for something on a deeper level.' If you can establish that spirit of openness and trust, even when passions are rising, then it can only inspire respect, whether or not things get physical.

> ❛ *It was animal attraction from start to finish . . . we all knew where this date was heading when they climbed into a taxi.* ❜

UP CLOSE & PERSONAL

YES, MISTRESS
SHIRLEY & DAVE

No stranger to over-sharing, Scouser Shirley, 54, freely confesses to exploring the dominant side of her sexuality. 'I've been approached by men who want to wear my panties and men who want to clean my house,' she says, 'which is a win-win, really.' Dave, 52, does his level best to blink, and from that moment on the table is set for frisky conversation that could well be heading in one direction. 'I do look awesome in latex,' she admits candidly, 'but you don't half sweat.' At this, Dave has heard quite enough. 'We should kick the arse out of a second date,' he suggests before the couple make their exit.

SEALED WITH A KISS
MARK & LOUISE

Funny, bright and breezy 44-year-old divorcée Louise arrives fully prepared to be disappointed. She's sick of attracting sexters, and beginning to give up hope of ever finding the man of her dreams. Enter strapping South African ex-soldier Mark, and Louise responds like the sun has just broken through the clouds for the first time in ages. Following a meal that sees an electric charge build up between the couple like rubbing a balloon on a jumper, we follow them to the bench on the terrace outside the restaurant – for some fresh air and the kind of steamy clinch you'd expect from two hormonally charged teens.

TRIPLE NAUGHTY EYES
CAMERON & LOUISA

Property surveyor Cameron is set to cook up chemistry with his date even if it doesn't exist naturally. When Louisa takes a loo break, he even tries out his technique on their waitress, CiCi. 'It's just something I do to create sexual tension,' he explains. 'You look in the left eye, and then the right eye, and then down to the lips,' he adds to finish. CiCi moves on with a chuckle, which leaves Cameron warmed up and ready to deploy what he calls the 'triple naughty eyes' just as soon as Louisa returns. With time together, it might've had a devastating impact – but not as much as seeing his card declined when it comes to paying the bill. 'It's probably better if we're like . . . friends?' Cameron offers afterwards, which might be optimistic.

MEET MY BICEPS
KENNY & CLAIRE

Having dated women for years, Claire now thinks about men 24/7. With a weakness for guys with big muscles, her jaw hits the restaurant floor when six-foot-six basketball player Kenny dips under the door frame. What's more, Kenny has brought two friends in tow – his biceps, 'James and Andrew'. While some girls might not be so easily impressed by his muscular mates, Claire can't resist touching as well as looking. The heat is on as the couple take to their table, where Kenny asks what type of man turns her on. Ignoring James and Andrew, Claire looks him directly in the eye and whispers, 'Men like you.'

❧ AND FINALLY ❧

You cannot deny sexual chemistry when it is there, but it should never be the main thing that holds your relationship together. It can be wonderful and wild and pleasurable, but all of those other things that bond you – like trust and respect – are far more important long term.

Without a doubt sexual chemistry creates fireworks. It can be dazzling and intense – and yes, you can both walk away with happy memories. But what is left when the last rocket has lit up the sky? That is where other elements come into play: from a shared smile to a sense of feeling complete in each other's company. As couples we forge our own connections. If we only focus on physical desire we risk losing sight of the smaller, quieter elements that can also prove so strong and enduring.

"

Passion is a sort of fever in the mind.

"

WILLIAM PENN

DATE LINES . . .

THEY SAID WHAT?

Find out who's behind these quotes
on page 251

12. 'I would love to find someone who I can just be me with all the time'

13. 'Mum says treat her like a lady. I'll pop down your chimney, innit!'

14. 'Comfortable? That's what you look for in a sofa'

15. 'Are you attracted to Alistair?'
    'You're talking about yourself in the third person'

16. 'Some guys have a bit of an edge to them. I have no edge. I'm a circle'

17. 'Love makes the world go round, whether it's a friendship sort of love or a love of pizza'

18. 'He's gorgeous. How can you not fancy this?'

19. 'Everyone tells me I look like Buzz Lightyear'
    'Oh, God. You do! Is that good?'
    'You tell me. Do you like a bit of toy action?'

20. 'You're gorgeous'
    'Pardon?'
    'You're my Coke and JD, cup and tea, bread and Nutella. Whatever . . .'

21. 'Well, I fancy you'
    'Oh, that's all right then. 'Cause I fancy you'
    'Sweet then, innit?'

Rules of Attraction

Chapter Twelve

THE POWER OF PERSONALITY

People are so interesting. Often they will say that they like something, but once they get it they aren't always sure that they still want it.

We all have an ideal in our heads of how we want someone to look, but sometimes you can have such a connection that your requirements are forgotten in an instant. You may even be drawn to the total opposite of what you had imagined.

Of course we all have a 'type' and a certain look we are excited by, but until you get to know someone you can't know if that's what you want or not. I have met some truly beautiful women over the years, but they have not had my attention for long if they don't have something more than looks to offer.

Sex is all in the mind and there has to be a connection up top for there to be a connection down below. As we discussed in Chapter 11 'Sexual Chemistry', you can have an incredible time with someone you have that fire with, but there must also be a mental connection for it to be something that will last.

There's a saying in France that goes 'Loin des yeux, loin du cœur', which translates as 'Far away from the eyes, far away from the heart'. That would imply that if someone is a distance from you, even if there is love, it will diminish over time. So there is this idea that you have to be close to people in order to love them more. Personally, if love is genuine no distance can break it because you have the other person in your heart.

If a relationship was just about looks how could that happen? If you were just with someone because of their appearance alone then you would lose interest if you didn't see them. It is the deeper bond and the closeness it brings that really matter. It is seeing who someone truly is.

> **There has to be a connection up top for there to be a connection down below.**

I have seen it so often in the restaurant. Two daters can be exactly what each other desires physically, but their personalities don't click. A diner will have a big smile on their face when their date walks in, but you can see the look of disappointment that emerges if that person is boring or rude.

Someone can go from being very attractive to quite unattractive without changing a single thing about themselves physically. A bad personality can strip someone of their nice clothes and expensive haircut in seconds. It is nice to look at someone who is physically gorgeous, but you cannot have a long-term relationship with someone who has no depth. If you have any kind of substance, someone who relies entirely on how they look will become tedious very quickly.

HOW WAS IT FOR YOU?

Sometimes you think you want a certain look or type, but then you realize it isn't what you want after all.'

After being single for six years, PA Lucy had a 'now or never' moment when she applied for *First Dates*. And she enjoyed the experience so much she came back for seconds.

Her debut date was with Sav, whose dazzling smile swiftly made him a firm Twitter favourite. 'I wasn't expecting to meet the person I was going to marry or anything when I applied for *First Dates*, but I had a lot of fun,' begins Lucy. 'My date with Sav was really good-looking and of course I found him attractive. Who wouldn't?'

Despite the physical attraction something didn't quite 'click' for Lucy, who reckons you have to look a lot deeper than a pretty face to find your perfect match. 'Sav had a good personality and as soon as we met I knew we'd get along and it wouldn't be awkward. But I felt like I had to be a bit different to how I'd normally be on a first date. I was very loud so I may have come across as a bit mouthy. I'm not sure why, but it felt more like we were having a laugh than flirting. I did fancy Sav but I couldn't see myself being with him. Something was definitely missing between us.'

When Lucy made her return to the *First Dates* restaurant she came out as gay and went on a date with outspoken Nicola. But despite finding Nicola attractive on sight, once again that essential magic was missing. 'I thought Nicola was attractive when I first met her, but the more I got to know her the less I fancied her. My perception of her changed when we chatted and I stopped fancying her pretty much straight away. I wanted to be myself but she made that difficult because I felt like she was sizing me up all the time. She didn't like my hair and tattoos, which made me feel self-conscious. I just thought, "Even if we do fancy each other loads, if you don't like certain things about me you're not for me because I do like those things."'

Lucy, 28, says she's met many people who are lovely looking on the outside, but if they reveal a hollow centre she's turned off in an instant. 'There has to be more to liking a person than just what you see. It can't be all about face value. I got chatting to a fit guy on Tinder a while ago and he sounded decent over text, but as soon as I spoke to him face-to-face I realized what an idiot he was. We went bowling and all he did was talk about himself. For ages. It didn't matter that he was gorgeous; he was sending me to sleep and it put me right off him.'

Looks don't always shine as brightly as we grow older, so Lucy reckons you need to focus on more than good hair and a pert bum when it comes to meeting your soulmate. 'You do need to find someone attractive to a certain extent, but as I'm getting older personality is becoming a priority. Let's face it, when you get to a certain age everything goes south and wrinkly, but your personality is never going to change. You're always going to be the person you are. So if you fall in love with someone for who they are and not because they've got an amazing body or nice teeth you'll do alright. Anyone can make themself a nine or ten with make-up, but once they take that make-up off they can slip down to a five or six pretty quickly. With a good filter and angle you can look a hell of a lot better online than you do in real life. I've been catfished quite a lot; I'll arrange to meet someone and when they turn up it's a shock. But if they're funny and we get on I don't mind that they don't look like that sculpted goddess profile picture. In fact, I wasn't instantly attracted to my last boyfriend but I ended up falling for his personality. His face didn't change but the way I looked at it did. Being nice and kind and funny can make someone very attractive.'

There can be a big difference between what you think you want and what you really need, so Lucy advises keeping an open mind. 'Sometimes you think you want a certain look or type but then you realize it isn't what you want after all. On paper I've always gone for girlie girls with dark hair and dark skin. But my last girlfriend had short blonde hair, a bit of a tomboy. I don't think you can pigeonhole potential partners. You might meet someone who is physically perfect for you, but it ends up being a pretty empty relationship.'

Lucy is still single but her appearances on *First Dates* sparked interest. 'A few girls got in touch with me after seeing me on the show so I have been on some dates. Whatever happens on a date I always try to be myself. I read the other day that when you go on a first date it's not you on that date, it's a representative, and that's true. I've been on dates before where I haven't been myself and I think that's put people off. If someone is going to fall for you they need to fall for everything about you. There's no point in pretending to be anyone other than yourself.'

> 6 *When you get to a certain age everything goes south and wrinkly, but your personality is never going to change.* 9

LAURA SAYS

I'm one of those people who believes that physical attraction isn't the only spark that you should be looking for on a first date. Having served so many tables where couples are getting to know each other, there's isn't always an instant connection between them. Sometimes, early on, one of them will make their excuses to go to the loo, and in passing they'll whisper to me that they're not feeling anything special about the person. My response is always the same: give it time.

Personality is the most attractive thing anyone has to offer. Sure, it helps if you're drawn to that person physically, but it's not always a deal breaker.

The key is what makes them tick on the inside, and that only becomes apparent as you talk about your lives, interests, hopes and dreams, and find you share a lot in common. As a result, a date can begin in quite a low-key way, without looking like anything promising is on the cards, and end up with the couple feeding each other across the table. As a classic example look at Sav and Lucy. Lucy is an outgoing woman with few reservations, and Sav is smart and funny. Conversation was always going to come naturally to them, but it didn't look like they fancied each other at first sight. That was something that seemed to develop over the meal as they talked and joked and drummed up more double entendres than most. As it turned out, Lucy returned to the restaurant sometime later to date another woman, but it was clear to us all that she and Sav were genuinely drawn to each other based on more than looks alone. Even though it didn't turn into a big romance, they still had a lot of fun together.

A first date is a simple way to work out if there's potential for romance. You don't have to be deeply attracted to that person to feel like a second date is worth a shot just to see where it takes you. It's a rare thing when two strangers meet in the restaurant and discover they are soulmates over drinks and life partners by dessert. It happens from time to time, but more often than not any instant connection is based on sexual chemistry. Feeling that physical pull is one thing, but any sense of deeper attraction always needs time to take root and grow. It may even take more than a second date for that to happen. So long as you're both enjoying the experience it can be even more rewarding than falling for someone in a heartbeat.

If you asked anyone to list the rules of attraction, they'd all come up with different things. That's the great thing about romance. There is no rule book. It's about going out to have a good time, and enjoying the company of someone you hope to get to know better. The only rule that can apply to everyone is to always be sure that you follow your heart.

> ❛ *Feeling that physical pull is one thing, but any sense of deeper attraction always needs time to take root and grow.* ❜

UP CLOSE & PERSONAL

DRESS TO IMPRESS
SAM & LIVVY

IT worker and self-confessed nerd Sam may be a whizz with computers, but his love life needs a reboot. He's a passionate guy with plenty of interests, and when Livvy arrives to find him deep in conversation at the bar with Merlin about favourite Marvel characters, it looks like he might've blown it before they've even begun. To everyone's surprise, not least our favourite geek, Livvy opens with the line, 'So where do you stand on cosplay?' When she reveals that she's into dressing up as *Game of Thrones*' Daenerys, Sam has to remind himself to breathe. 'Wow,' is all he can say, and we just know this is going to work out wonderfully before they've even ordered from the menu. 'You're a complete dork,' Livvy tells him afterwards, 'and I love that.'

SMART THINKING
RICH & KERRY

'Women still terrify me a little bit,' admits ginger gent Rich, 31, who is fresh from a long-term relationship and steeling himself for the evening ahead with a lemonade at the bar. When flame-haired Scottish maiden Kerry walks into the restaurant, Rich quickly recognizes he has nothing to fear. Even her membership of elite brainbox club Mensa doesn't faze him, and the couple soon get on famously over a shared love of frozen pizza and soppy adverts. Even when Rich discovers he can't quite foot the bill he's so generously offered to pay, Kerry is more than happy to spare his blushes and focus on the fact that they'd love to see each other again.

SIGNS OF LOVE
PATRICK & WAYNE

Patrick, 23, only went public about his sexuality a year ago. Nervously, he broke the news to his mum first, who promptly threw him a 'coming-out barbecue'. Despite such overwhelming support, he's still finding his feet on the dating scene. In walks sunny Brummie Wayne, 24, and Patrick's face lights up. What follows is a meal marked by lots of laughter and adoring looks, and it's lovely to see Patrick blossom before our eyes. Finally, this perfect match is sealed with a lesson in signing from Wayne (born to deaf parents) who teaches him how to say, 'You have beautiful eyes,' in the most genuine and touching way.

CHEMICAL REACTION
ASHLEY & SONIA

Geordie singleton Sonia is on a quest to find her Prince Charming. Until now, however, her dates have headed for the hills when they find out she's a single mum. Now she's hoping for a change in fortune over dinner with brawny 27-year-old Ashley. He might be an unlikely-

looking scientist, but when Sonia learns that he's keen to settle down and have kids she practically bubbles over with excitement. As the elements of love come together over dessert, the couple even go so far as to contemplate running off to Gretna Green.

❧ AND FINALLY ❧

The one thing that doesn't change as we get older is our personality and our goodness. Time may take smooth skin and give us wrinkles, but it rewards us with wisdom and a good heart, and this is when we can truly appreciate the rules of attraction.

When we're young it is easy to think that attraction is all about looks. Over time, and with experience, we come to appreciate what makes someone truly special. It can mean different things to different people, of course, but I would sum it up as a beauty of spirit. From the warmth of their smile, sense of humour or generous nature, this is the source of a deeper, enduring attraction that can bind two people together for life.

"

All our souls
are written
in our eyes.

"

EDMOND ROSTAND
CYRANO DE BERGERAC

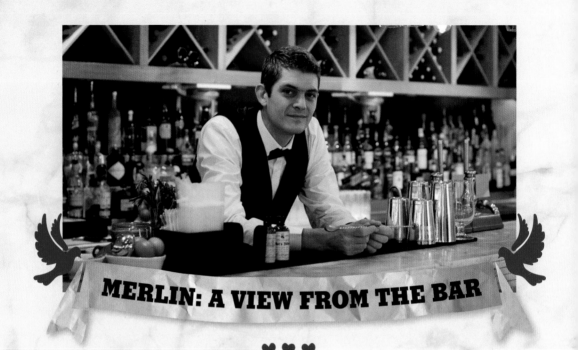

MERLIN: A VIEW FROM THE BAR

♥ ♥ ♥

‘ *A good barman listens more than he talks.* ’

Working in the *First Dates* restaurant is different to any other job I've had. Usually as a bar tender you want regulars: people who come back again and again. But generally in the *First Dates* restaurant if you don't see someone again it means the date has worked out, which is what we're aiming for. I only really want to see them again if they've got some good news to tell us.

Normally in a restaurant you're running a fast service, turning over tables quickly, and the whole day slips past in a bit of a blur. Conversely, what we do on *First Dates* is try to keep people there for as long as possible in the hope the date will go well.

I serve all the daters that come in, not just the ones who are shown on TV, so I am kept busy, but I'm always on hand to lend an ear if people are nervous or want someone to talk to. People often think I dish out words of wisdom behind the bar, but I'm the last person who should give out dating advice! I've been in a relationship for eleven years now so I'm a bit out of touch with modern dating. But if it helps someone when they have a chat to me, that's great. A good barman listens more than he talks, and I'm there as a catalyst to encourage conversations.

Sometimes the first dater to arrive will be waiting at the bar for half an hour to forty-five minutes so I do get to have a good chat with them. Most people are really nervous, of course, and a drink helps them to relax a bit more. When the second dater arrives I get them a drink and then step back, because I don't want to be a third wheel. Sometimes I won't even get a chance to offer them a drink because the daters are so into each other I won't get a look-in. I love that, because it means the couple are really hitting it off.

That initial moment at the bar is when the daters are going to find out a lot about each other in a short space of time. I've only stepped in once or twice to help a couple out – if the conversation isn't flowing, or things seem awkward. I usually ask them if they want a drink, to change the topic and give them something new to talk about.

> ❛ We've already met our perfect date and we know them intimately because they are literally in our dreams. It's just a case of being able to meet them in real life. ❜

I would never interrupt someone's flow if two people are getting on well, because it's rude, but if I think people are struggling I'll subtly help them out. We're there to create an environment for people to get together, so sometimes I'll attempt to derail a bad conversation so they can pick it up from somewhere else. As I've chatted to one dater before the other has arrived I'll also know a bit about them, and it may be that I can interject something interesting about them and steer a conversation back into the right gear.

In my opinion the most successful daters are the people who have a clear idea of what they think is missing from their lives. We've all got a sense of a life unlived and a mental picture of the perfect partner, and that relates very closely to who you want to meet. There's an idea that we've already met our perfect date and we know them intimately because they are literally in our dreams. It's just a case of being able to meet them in real life.

There is never a dull moment in the *First Dates* bar. It was great when Lucy, who was a weightlifter, picked me up. It's not often you get hoisted into the air by a customer. I also love it when we get real characters in, like Jodie the postwoman. Good moments at the bar are made by people like her. She was happy to chat away about everything without any reservations, and it was utterly brilliant. People like her make our job so much fun.

I enjoy the livelier dates, and you can always tell which ones those are going to be because they start with shots. It always makes me smile and I think, 'OK, I can see which way this date is going!' Funnily enough, Adam and Dan kicked off with shots of sambuca. That was Adam's idea. He looked at Dan and said, 'Cheeky sambuca?' and they were away.

Some people do tip over the edge with drinking. Anna was determined to put her best foot forward but she drank a lot because she was worried about the evening. I thought she was brilliant, though. Often when people come back to the restaurant a second or third time because dates haven't worked, they'll think it's a problem with them and they'll try and change their personality to suit other people. Anna didn't do that. She stuck to her principles and she still had a drink the second time around, and she was totally herself. She's happy with who she is and she knows there's someone out there who will like her exactly the way she is. She isn't going to change for anyone.

On the flip side, another one of my favourite daters was Luke. He was a proper West London geezer and he had a rotten first date. He came back for the second date and he smartened himself up and toned things down a bit, and the date went much better. On the third date he was like a different person. You could tell he'd decided he really wanted to be in a relationship and it was like he gave himself a crash course in dating. His attitude totally changed and his final date went tremendously. I love the fact that if a date doesn't work out people will pick themselves up and come back again. It's brave enough to go to the *First Dates* restaurant once, but coming back takes a lot of courage.

The older couples always make me smile. Billy and Sandra, and Terence and Olive, were amazing; Billy started dancing in the restaurant. It's a different level of bravery to date when you get older. I've chatted to some of the older guys and asked them why they've decided to come to the restaurant and they've all pretty much said the same: 'What have I got to lose?' That's such a good attitude. Love isn't just about big explosions and grand gestures; it's about companionship, too. It's very heart-warming and life-affirming to see those couples working out.

I've learned to take everything in my stride working behind the bar, but I'm always so shocked when people stand someone up. I think that's such a terrible thing to do and I can't understand why anyone would be so inconsiderate. If you've gone as far as to commit and arrange to meet someone, you should follow the date through. Or certainly tell them upfront that you don't want to go on the date any more. It's not rocket science. Georgia got stood up and she was such a lovely girl and came across so well. I really hope the guy who was supposed to date her watched the show afterwards and kicked himself. All I can do when someone gets stood up is try to make them feel comfortable. We do all we can as a team to make sure they still enjoy their evening.

> **6 The older couples always make me smile . . . Love isn't just about big explosions and grand gestures; it's about companionship, too. 9**

It's always really interesting when we get famous people in the restaurant, and it's great that they get set up with someone who isn't famous. It must be so strange when a dater arrives and they're, like, 'Hang on, my date's Anthea Turner!' But at the end of the day, famous or not, we all have similar wants and desires, regardless of what we do for a living. It's interesting to be able to chat to people in the public eye and find out about the person behind the public persona, because often it's a fantasy construct. Sometimes you get someone who is very similar to how they're portrayed in the media and sometimes someone is totally different, and it's important to realize they're no different to anyone else just because they're well known. We all want to find love – whether we're a superstar, or we work in a supermarket.

Working with Sam, CiCi and Laura is such a hoot. Sam has one of the most lateral minds I've ever come across. He makes these incredible intuitive jumps from subject to subject and he's one of my favourite people I've ever worked with. And it turns out he's a mean juggler. I started doing a bit of juggling behind the bar when I had quiet moments, and then Sam started doing it and he was amazing. He's circus level. A beer with Fred at the end of a busy *First Dates* night is always a winner for me, too. Once the doors have closed, and it's all done and dusted, a quick drink and a chat before we hit the road is a great way to wind down. And we've always got plenty to talk about.

Made in Heaven

Chapter Thirteen

ON SOULMATES

Faith in love is wonderful, but you have to be aware that it can hurt sometimes if your expectations are too high.

I don't think you can expect someone to be your lover, your best friend, and do your washing, take you out for dinner, and buy you presents. That person doesn't exist, and a soulmate is not about finding someone who is 'perfect'. It is about finding someone who is perfect for you. This means you have to be realistic in love. You cannot hope to meet a great-looking billionaire who will fall madly in love with you, and then feel disappointed if you only meet an average-looking millionaire.

Do I believe that there is just one person for everyone? I would say not, because otherwise you will always be searching for that one person who has all the qualities you desire and you may miss out on someone else who is amazing. Or you could be on your own for ever. Fifty per cent of couples divorce, so if all of those couples have found 'the One' and then they split up does that mean they have to be alone for ever because no one else will be right? You may think there is just one special someone for you but there are six billion people in the world, so what about the others?

Some people will meet and have everything the other one wants, but then something won't click and there will be no passion. And other people will meet and already know they want to be with that person. Maybe we just need the one for now, and something more can grow?

Don't search for the impossible. Compromise doesn't mean settling. The definition of compromise is 'an agreement or settlement of a dispute that is reached by each side making concessions'. That means not having it all your own way. So you can't have a checklist for everything. There will always be something – a quirk or a habit – that you may not like but you can accept. Compromise is not just about dark or light hair, or where you go on holiday; it is about the relationship as a whole.

You will never know whether someone is everything you want on the very first date. They may have a lot of the qualities you are looking for and you may find them very attractive, but that is very much about the surface. It is only when you dig a little deeper and get to know someone for real that you truly know if they are the one for you.

You don't want to put the cart before the horse. You may meet someone who ticks all the right boxes, but don't leap in. Be prudent. What looks good on paper doesn't always translate well to real life.

> **You will never know whether someone is everything you want on the very first date.**

HOW WAS IT FOR YOU?

ADAM

DAN

'Dan proposed by putting a ring in my Christmas stocking.'

Having been single for eight and a half years, desperate Dan dreamed of meeting the right man. But when he applied for *First Dates* on a whim he didn't expect to find himself planning a wedding a few months later. 'I was in bed after watching *First Dates* with a bottle of wine and I thought, "Why can't I meet the right man?"' says the Sunderland native. 'So I got my laptop out and applied there and then.'

Meanwhile, his future fiancé, Adam, was 250 miles away in Bury St Edmunds doing exactly the same thing. And the date was set sooner than both thought. 'I couldn't believe it when they told me,' Adam laughs. 'I thought I'd be waiting for ages, and it all happened so quickly I didn't have time to think about it. It wasn't until I was standing at King's Cross train station on my way to the date that I thought, "What the hell am I doing?"'

What he was doing was heading to meet his future husband – only he didn't know it just yet. 'I just wanted to meet someone I got on with and could have a laugh with,' says Dan. 'I honestly didn't think that I could end up meeting the person I was going to spend the rest of my life with.'

And initially, communication manager Dan wasn't certain he had. 'When I walked in and saw Adam he was so muscly and manly. He was drinking a pint and I thought, "Well, this date isn't going to last for very long. He's not going to fancy me,"' says the 42-year-old. 'But as soon as I sat down the conversation flowed straight away. We talked about why we'd applied for the show and where we were from. I laughed a lot when Adam described himself as a classy stripper because he "never takes his pants off".'

The pair were so enthralled with each other they lost track of time, and had to be politely asked to leave the restaurant. 'We thought we'd only been there for about an hour and we hadn't had our dessert or anything, but the restaurant was about to close,' explains Adam. 'We looked at our watches and we couldn't believe how long we'd been chatting. We talked about everything and anything. There wasn't a single uncomfortable silence. It just felt right. I know it sounds corny but we just stared into each other's eyes the whole time.'

After sharing their first kiss on Platform 4 of King's Cross Station they kept in touch daily, and fate brought them together the following week. 'I've never had to work in Ipswich before in my entire life, but the week after our date I had to go there for an event and stay over,' says Dan. 'It was so strange that I happened to be down the road from Adam, and we had four dates that week. It was like we'd known one another for years and it still feels like that now. We spend loads of time with each other's friends and we kind of fill in each other's gaps when we're talking.'

Do they share passions and interests? 'We've got a lot in common, and we've got a lot not in common,' reveals Adam. 'Dan is a huge *Doctor Who* fan and when I went to his house for the first time and saw his *Doctor Who*-themed office I was taken aback. We bicker every now and again like an old married couple do, but we've never had a proper argument. I can't understand why I would argue with him. There's nothing for us to fall out over. Maybe if we were more similar we'd argue because we'd both have firm ideas about how things should be done, but it's our differences that work.'

Dan agrees that opposites attract. 'We've got a lot in common, like we both love movies, going to the cinema and socializing, but we're also opposites in some ways. I'm into technology and Adam isn't, so if something goes wrong with his phone I'll fix it. But he's much more practical, so he takes care of DIY stuff. He likes to live in a tidy house but he's not tidy, so I make sure the house always looks nice. You don't have to love everything each other does to be right for each other. Dan is never going to read Spider-Man comics before bed like I do, and I'm never going to be a whizz at painting walls. But we open each other up to new experiences and we learn a lot from each other.'

> **6 Part of the reason our attraction was so instant is that we were totally ourselves. 9**

Dan popped the big question to Adam on Christmas Day 2015, which also happened to be decorator Adam's fortieth birthday, and they're now busy planning their big day. 'I knew I wanted to spend the rest of my life with Adam,' says Dan. 'He'd always said he wasn't going to get married, but I kept everything crossed that he'd change his mind. I was 99.9 percent sure he would say yes to my proposal but I was still so nervous. I even got his dad's permission and he gave me his blessing.'

'Of course I said yes straight away,' smiles Adam. 'Dan proposed by putting a ring in my Christmas stocking and it was an amazing moment. We're so happy together and part of the reason our attraction was so instant is that we were totally ourselves, and we liked each other for who we really were. Neither of us were trying to impress the other one or put on an act; we were completely genuine. We've always been totally honest with each other, and that's so important.'

'I just knew it was right when we met,' continues Dan. 'It's worth waiting for your Prince Charming to come along, because he will.'

CICI SAYS

The moment Dan walked through the restaurant door, I could read his lips when he looked across to the bar, saw his date, and just went, 'Wow.' There was nothing restrained about it, as if he was allowing himself to be entranced and impressed.

It was lovely, because as a singleton in that situation you often want to hide how you're truly feeling. You don't know this person, after all, which means you risk coming across as a bit intense or needy if you're openly that attracted to them. In this case, Dan was totally transparent and Adam just went with it. There was something very special about this couple. They had sparkle.

I'm often asked if I can tell whether a couple are made for each other. Sam just laughs before I've answered, because he knows what a romantic I can be about these things. I'm just one of those girls who loves a fairy-tale ending. It doesn't always happen, of course, and sometimes it takes time for two people to recognize they've found each other. But I think even Sam would agree that with Adam and Dan we just knew it was going to work out right from the start.

In the *First Dates* restaurant couples are often very aware of their surroundings. As a result they tend to look around a lot. Dan and Adam were different. Once they'd settled at their table it was as if they had climbed inside their personal bubble. They were just completely unaware of what was going on around them. When I served them they were impeccably polite and charming, but didn't stop looking at each other. These guys were locked in as a couple, and the conversation flowed. It was a beautiful thing to watch unfolding.

Adam and Dan were the very definition of a perfect match. It's always interesting to ask what makes a couple like this work so well. At the restaurant, a great deal of effort goes into pairing people in the hope that it'll be a success, but there's no magic formula. We can serve up a blind date that might tick every box on paper, and yet face-to-face there's something missing. Often, it isn't something that anyone can put into words, but it can make or break the date. We're talking about chemistry, and no amount of matchmaking can conjure it up. All we can do is create the right environment for a blind date and let destiny take its course. And when everything comes together across that candlelit table, it's a wonderful thing.

UP CLOSE & PERSONAL

THE ZOMBIE BOND
LACHLAN & BECCA

The stakes are high for Lachlan, returning for his second stab at finding love. But in the mind of this self-confessed nerd, the kind of stakes that spring to his mind in conversation with psychologist Becca are sharpened in readiness for the zombie apocalypse. 'Head north,' he advises her, 'because there are farms and there are going to be guns.' As Lachlan holds forth on his carefully considered survival strategy, many girls might be metaphorically heading home, but not Becca. Why? Because Lachlan has tapped into her personal passion, and the couple bond over ways to stay alive together when the undead roam the earth. Sweet.

HEAVEN CAN WAIT
BILLY & SANDRA

Sandra loves to dance, though her former husband preferred to stand on the sidelines – even on their wedding day. While many old romantics might consider moving on to a club with a dance floor, widower Billy seizes the moment and invites his dinner

date to step out for a twirl in the restaurant itself. Flanked by Fred, the couple make the most of the opportunity, and by turns it becomes apparent to one and all that this charming couple have found a soulmate in each other. Such is the bond that Billy and Sandra even return to the restaurant at Christmas.

GOOD THING GOING
MICHAEL & KARINA

Here are two lonely hearts in search of a lucky break. Both Michael and Karina have had bad experiences on the dating scene, and it's rocked their confidence. 'I'm starting to wonder if there's something wrong with me,' laughs Karina beforehand, while Michael waits anxiously at the

bar. As it turns out, their fortunes are about to turn. Cupid doesn't just look kindly on the pair but ensures an evening of good humour and flirtation. Even Karina's profession as a stripper doesn't faze our man, who continues to make her laugh all the way out to the taxi and a ride into town for more drinks.

ON GUARD
MARCUS & CLAUDIA

Claudia arrives for her date with her sister in tow. She's had a tough time on the dating scene, and so her guard is up and she needs the moral support. Fortunately, her dining companion is all-round nice guy Marcus. Slowly, as the couple get to know each other,

her barriers begin to drop. Romance is in the air for sure, as Fred observes when he attends to their table. 'I think you're well-matched together, *non?*' he tells them, and Marcus agrees completely. Being a gent, he gives Claudia every chance to finish the date as friends . . . but she shares his affections wholeheartedly.

❦ AND FINALLY ❦

A relationship cannot exist without compromise.
We are complicated creatures who are always
changing and evolving, so our relationships do too.

As long as you have love and you have
understanding, you are in a good place.

Perfection doesn't make a relationship perfect. Hard
work, shared respect, understanding and a willingness to
compromise are what make it magical. Through my eyes
that is how two people in a loving relationship can become
stronger as individuals. And it can't get better than that.

66

*Love is composed
of a single soul
inhabiting two bodies.*

99

ARISTOTLE

Made in Hell

Chapter Fourteen

NOTHING VENTURED, NOTHING GAINED

Not all dates can be amazing. In the same way that you can feel when someone is right for you straight away, there will be times when you can tell when someone is not right for you. But of course you can't just turn around and walk out the door as soon as you get there, because that would be very unkind.

You don't want to be the reason why someone shies away from love even more.

The most important thing is not to hurt someone. There is no need to be unnecessarily rude, abrupt and unpleasant.

Some of the people who come to the *First Dates* restaurant have been traumatized and they've lost their trust in relationships, and they have problems with sharing themselves and connecting with others. They always remain on their guard and alone because they don't believe there is someone out there for them. You don't want to be the reason why someone shies away from love even more.

If you are desperate to leave the date and you can't bear to see it through to the end, the key is to communicate your intentions in advance and be careful how you word the fact that you want to leave. This way, your departure doesn't take the other person by surprise. Be polite but clear, and thank them for their time. At the end of the day you may be feeling bad about leaving early, but they may be secretly hoping you do.

If your date suggests taking the evening on, and you're not keen, just say you're sorry but you have to go. Then text them later and say it was lovely to meet them but you don't think things are going to go any further. It is much kinder to be upfront.

You can usually tell if someone is not interested in you. Ultimately, you should respect that, even if you think they are the most wonderful person you've ever met. You don't want it to become uncomfortable for either of you if they make it obvious they are itching for the exit. If your date is trying to get away, please don't try and make them stay. Cut your losses and put your energy into your next (hopefully much better) date.

If you are worried about how a date will go before you even arrive, aim to have a firm idea about how you are going to spend the evening. If you know you don't want to stay all night, plan when you want to go home so you can excuse yourself and end on a positive note.

Whatever happens, don't get your friend to phone you and then make an excuse. Everyone knows about that trick now, and people are too smart for it. It is better to be honest than pretend there is some kind of family emergency. Let someone down with dignity.

HOW WAS IT FOR YOU?

PADDY

'*I didn't expect to break the Internet.*'

When you go along for a date hoping to meet the woman of your dreams, the last thing you expect to do is cause a Twitter meltdown. But that's exactly what happened when 43-year-old Paddy met 37-year-old Heather. 'I'd been single for about a year following a long-term relationship and so I was well happy when I had a chance to visit the *First Dates* restaurant. Heather and I definitely didn't hit it off, though. In fact, it was quite the opposite.'

Not hitting it off is something of an understatement, but graphic designer Paddy was determined to try and make the best of a bad situation. 'Heather and I just weren't right for each other. We both knew that from the moment we arrived. There was a weird atmosphere between us and it was like we were just going through the motions. When she told me she had a work diary and a dating diary, that was it for me. Who does that? I did think about walking out, but I thought it would be out of order so I stayed and saw it through.'

After cracking a few jokes and trying to make conversation with Heather – buoyed up by several beers and a few glasses of prosecco – Paddy decided to try and liven up the evening by shocking her as much as possible. 'I was trying to have a nice time with Heather but she didn't seem at all interested and kept shutting me down every time I asked her a question. I don't think I went to the gym enough for her, because she's into muscly blokes. I got quite tiddly and I was rambling on and I thought, "Ah well, I'll have some fun and speak my mind." When Heather mentioned she was vegetarian, and said she doesn't eat meat or fish, it sparked off an innuendo in my mind. I tried to hold it back but I managed to last about a second before I made a comment about fish and an ex-girlfriend of mine.'

And just in case you didn't fully get the gist from Paddy's explanation, here's that controversial quote in full: 'I was seeing this girl who was quite domineering, she was scary. I won't go into any more details because it's quite personal. But it stank. And you don't like fish.'

Paddy insists it was all meant as a bit of fun but Heather wasn't exactly killing herself laughing. 'People who know me know I'm just messing about and I'm not out to offend anyone. It was a tongue-in-cheek comment,' explains Paddy. 'I'm always coming out with stupid stuff like that and it's only a bit of a laugh. Heather looked horrified.'

As were many viewers, who took to Twitter to discuss Paddy's comments; #fishgate was trending. 'I didn't expect to break the Internet. People went a bit mad for it and it was all over Twitter. I got slated, but I also got quite a lot of love. Some people thought it was funny and some were disgusted.'

Funnily enough, the couple weren't rushing to set up a second date. 'When I was asked after dinner if I wanted to see Heather again, I said "definitely". Clearly I was being sarcastic. I also said I was going to go home and do twenty naked star jumps because she's into fit guys. I don't regret anything I said on the show. I was only having a laugh and the last thing I'd want to do is offend anyone. I couldn't wait to get out of the restaurant, but my umbrella had disappeared and it was pouring with rain. I was more annoyed about that than my date with Heather not working out.'

Heather hasn't been Paddy's only nightmare lady encounter, and one bad experience left the dad of two with a broken toilet. Thankfully he's now settled down, so dodgy dates are a thing of the past. 'I had a date with a girl who got so drunk she threw up in my toilet, and then fell over and destroyed my toilet seat. Now I've found a brilliant lady that I'm completely in love with and I'm very happy. She doesn't mind my stupid humour. It's such a relief as I won't have to go on another blind date. It's probably a relief for a lot of women, too. I'd love to say I could offer someone some advice about dating but I don't think I'm in much of a position to. Maybe just keep your mouth shut? And don't get too drunk, because you end up talking utter rubbish.'

> **6** *Don't get too drunk, because you end up talking utter rubbish.* **9**

SAM SAYS

The situation with Paddy and Heather was pretty awful. The chemistry wasn't there and things just went from bad to worse. It was pretty obvious there was no likelihood of a second date so Paddy decided to have a bit of a laugh instead.

We've all been on bad dates but it's how you handle them that's important. Just because you don't fancy someone it doesn't mean the entire evening has to go to pot. If the food's nice and the atmosphere is good you can still have a good time. Having said that, if someone is feeling awkward and they're making it obvious they'd rather be at home in front of the TV with a takeaway, there isn't any coming back from that.

If someone would rather be anywhere but with you – and they're not hiding it – it's going to make you feel uncomfortable. That's what happened with Heather and Paddy to a certain extent. Heather wasn't engaged, so Paddy decided to make a bit of a story out of the night. What he said about his ex was talked about for days afterwards. Everyone was so shocked they couldn't help but chat about it to their mates.

They weren't right for each other but it would have been nicer if they'd been respectful to each other and made the effort to make the evening enjoyable anyway. It felt like they'd both given up quite early on. It's horrible when that happens because you have the whole meal to get through. The best thing to do would be to find some common ground so you can at least have a good chat.

❛ *It felt like they'd both given up quite early on.* ❜

I've been lucky that I haven't had many bad dates; I try and make them fun, even if I know it's not going to lead to romance. If I do end up on a dodgy date in the future I think the polite thing to do will be to see it out until the end. It's a bit dramatic to halt the date halfway through the meal and do a runner. Imagine what that could do to the other person's confidence. Make a polite excuse to leave after dinner once the evening is naturally coming to a close.

I'm not saying you have to stay all night if you're having a terrible time. If you know there's no way you can make the best of it don't prolong the agony too much. Maybe just have one course instead of three.

UP CLOSE & PERSONAL

SAY MY NAME
FRANKIE & LAURA

Over dinner, Irish fashionista Laura begins to think her date is more interested in himself, and the waitresses, than he is in her. Slowly, her smile tightens as Frankie and his sculpted eyebrows keep the spotlight on his side of the table. As far

as Laura's concerned, she could place a mirror in her chair and he wouldn't notice that she'd gone. 'What's my name?' she asks afterwards. 'What's mine?' Frankie counters in a moment of bluster, and then realizes there's no escape. 'Siobhan?' he offers meekly, and can't contain his surprise and delight when she tells him that's correct. Our girl then plays him like a mouse under her paw, only to drop her smile for a murderous glare and the fabulous sign-off, 'It's Laura, you f***er.'

BAD DATE
SAV & CAT

On paper, Sav could prove to be the handsome prince that Cat has been waiting for. In her experience, previous contenders have always turned into frogs at the first kiss. Sav is looking suave, naturally charming, and least likely to disappoint, but Cat has exacting standards. Admitting to being 'a bit difficult at times', she promptly weighs into her date – from his choice of roll-neck jumper to his topics of conversation – and effectively chews up the poor man along with her meal. 'So can you grow to like someone?' he asks, clutching at straws over dessert. Cat spells out her answer afterwards, when asked if she'd see Sav again. 'No,' she says, and that's her final word.

ONE-WAY DATING
RHYS & GEORGIA

Nanny Georgia knows how to make a strong impression on a first date. It's all 'hair, nails and tan', as well as non-stop talking about life as she sees it. Georgia kicks off by asking her date, Rhys, about himself. He manages to squeeze in that he's a student, and off she goes. Not just at the bar but throughout the meal, from her schooling to her dinner preferences, her holidays and phobia of fish. Afterwards, when asked if they'd see each other again, Rhys indicates his preference with a subtle but pleading shake of the head.

AWKWARD TURTLE & AWKWARD TURKEY
LEE & RALPH

When asked if they'll see each other again, restaurant returnees Lee and Ralph burst out laughing. At the same time, they make no eye contact whatsoever, and have already gone their separate ways in spirit. So what went so wrong? 'He's just a know-it-all,' complains Lee, having snuck out for a ciggie and the chance to phone a friend. 'Plus he doesn't know who Sticky Vicky is.' While Ralph is unaware that Lee has dismissed their date as 'boring, morbid and depressing', he picks up on the vibe as they await the big question, and evidently shares the same sentiment. So at least they had one thing in common.

◈ AND FINALLY ◈

If you find yourself on a terrible date be as nice and considerate as you can, even if the other person turns out to be a nightmare. Take the higher ground and you will be able to walk away with dignity, and even earn their respect.

In my mind, there is no such thing as a bad date. It is about experience, and that is a valuable lesson. What matters is that you can be yourself, and look back knowing that you handled a difficult situation to the very best of your abilities.

Even if things don't work out, life is too short for regrets. We can learn a great deal from an unsuccessful date – not just about what we're seeking, but about who we are inside.

"

Everything has beauty, but not everyone sees it.

"

CONFUCIUS

Stood Up

♥

Chapter Fifteen

IT'S NOT YOU . . .

Being stood up is always going to be disappointing, but you can't take it personally. Instead, you have to remember that it is simply in some people's nature to let others down. I am very lucky that it has never happened to me, but I know many people who have been in that unfortunate situation.

If it is a first date, remember that it is not you they're standing up, because they don't know you. They're not rejecting you as a person; they've just lost their bottle, or they are not terribly nice. People do things for all sorts of reasons, and sometimes those reasons don't make sense.

We don't all have the same reality. Some people think it is OK to be a no-show and won't give it a second thought. But if you are a moral person who would never do such a thing then it can feel confusing and hurtful. If someone decides to disrespect you in that way it can also make you feel angry. And you are completely justified in feeling like that.

A phone call or a text takes a matter of minutes, so there is absolutely no excuse. However, it does you one favour: it clearly shows that you are not compatible with that person. Letting someone down is unkind and exhibits a lack of respect, but at the end of the day wouldn't you rather you found out someone was like that from the word go? Imagine if you started having a relationship with a person and then found out that they were ignorant and always put themself first. That would be horrible.

You must try not to let one bad experience traumatize you. It would be such a shame if being stood up made someone lose faith in human nature or question their ability to meet someone wonderful and be loved.

> ❛ *Letting someone down is unkind and exhibits a lack of respect.* ❜

It is like if a friend ripped you off and you lost £2,000; it is worth losing that money to know they're not a friend worth having. In my opinion that is good value. That has happened to me before, and seeing someone's true colours is priceless. I'm grateful every time it happens, because it means I can make more space for the good people in my life.

Sometimes people will disappoint you and you've got to roll with the punches. You must get straight back up and be strong. It is horrible having to break the news to people in the restaurant that their date has decided not to come, and there is no nice way to do it.

In my opinion the best way to deal with being stood up is to laugh it off, remember how incredible you are, and then go on a date with someone much better.

HOW WAS IT FOR YOU?

SASHA

'Right from the outset, I didn't think he was going to show up.'

As a rule, any singleton who walks through the *First Dates* restaurant door brings high hopes for the evening ahead. It is only natural to want to discover a soulmate across that candlelit table, and leave in the first flush of love. For London-based businesswoman Sasha, 25, that sense of optimism began to fade long before her arrival. 'I've always had quite a bad experience with men,' explains this graceful, raven-haired hopeful who won the hearts and the sympathy of a nation as well as the affections of a certain waiter. 'I also tend to blame myself for things going wrong,' she admits. 'As the evening approached, it became like a self-fulfilling prophecy. Of course, I wanted to find that perfect man, but in my mind I started thinking if something's going to go wrong then it's bound to happen to me. I figured my date wouldn't like me, and yes, the possibility that he wouldn't even show up crossed my mind. In a way,' she adds with disarming cheeriness, 'I was ready.'

Finding herself the first to arrive didn't bode well for Sasha. 'I had hoped to find my date waiting for me,' she says. 'As soon as I saw that empty bar stool, I began to prepare myself for the worst.' From that moment on, time seemed to tick more slowly. 'I was there for about twenty minutes, but it felt like two hours. Then Fred told me that my date was running late and that's when I began to doubt it was going to happen.'

So how does it feel to be the one left waiting while you're surrounded by couples enjoying dates? 'I wanted to cry,' confesses Sasha. 'It's humiliating. Nobody wants to be stood up, after all, and I had to give myself a bit of a talking to. At one point I took some time out in the Ladies. I remember passing Sam as I headed in, and catching his eye. I didn't think anything of it. In fact, when I returned to the bar I spotted him chatting to his colleagues. As they were glancing in my direction, I knew they were talking about me. I just assumed it was because I'd evidently been stood up.'

Despite feeling so self-conscious, alone at the bar in a restaurant hosting couples at candlelit tables, Sasha refused to run and hide. 'It was tough, but part of me kept saying I shouldn't just give up on the situation,' she says. 'I told myself to stay calm and see what happens.' Eventually, as the clock hands kept turning, Sasha took herself outside for fresh air and a cigarette. 'I only smoke when I'm seriously stressed,' she laughs, which at least meant she was in a good place when Fred followed her out to break the news that the date wasn't going to happen. 'Apparently, the guy had switched off his phone,' she says. 'By then, I didn't even want him to show up. It's just not a chivalrous way to behave after all the courage and effort it takes in going on a blind date. Sure, he might've been nervous, or changed his mind, but to vanish like that was selfish. I was angry, but above all I just felt disappointed.'

From an outside point of view, it's easy to feel nothing but sympathy for anyone who's been abandoned on a date. After all, it says more about the individual who's failed to show than it does for the one left with ice cubes melting in an empty glass. For that person, however, it's only natural to feel as if they're the centre of attention for all the wrong reasons, so when waiter Sam plucked up the courage to step outside and chat, Sasha's guard was up. 'I didn't find him crazily attractive,' she admits. 'But then we started talking and I got a sense of being rescued from the moment. It was a good feeling, especially when Sam asked to knock off early to spend time with me. He was complimentary throughout, and very good company, and that's when he began to seriously get my attention.'

While this moment of serendipity appeared to set up one of the show's most unexpected romances, Sasha didn't quite see it in the same way. 'Everyone, from my mum to my friends, said that we were made for each other,' she says. 'I guess we were caught up in a moment, and while it really was genuine and special I had just been through an emotionally draining experience.'

> 6 *It's his loss, because the experience has made me a lot more confident.* 9

Of course, there's only one question everyone's been asking Sasha since Cupid took pity on her as she smoked in solitude outside the restaurant. 'I did agree to see Sam again,' she says, with a smile, on finally setting the story straight. 'I was hopeful about the possibility of a romance, but cautious. I'd been stung, after all. Then a few weeks passed by before he called, and it just came too late. We went out, and had a lovely time. Sam even came round and cooked a meal for my flatmate and me, but by then it was clear we were just meant to be friends.'

As for the guy who failed to show up at all, Sasha looks back on the evening with a wise head on her shoulders. 'If he hadn't been such a coward, things might've been very different,' she says. 'If you don't put yourself out there, you're never going to meet anyone, and that's such a shame. It's his loss, because the experience has made me a lot more confident. I had to dig deep to get through it, and Sam's attention helped me to recognize at a low moment that I still had something to offer. In fact,' she finishes, 'I should be grateful to my blind date for not showing up, because otherwise I might never have had such a great evening with someone so genuinely warm and kind.'

CICI SAYS

From the moment it became clear that her date wasn't going to show, Sasha tried so hard to put on a brave face. Being stood up leaves you feeling deeply vulnerable, and she did an amazing job of staying strong.

Sasha's also a stunning woman. I asked Sam what he thought of her when we were serving tables. He wasn't going to be drawn, but he'd obviously noticed her because the next thing I know he was outside chatting. He's a natural with women – relaxed and good company. I could tell something was happening because her body language changed; she seemed to warm to his presence and gravitate across the sofa towards him, which was lovely to see. Sam was buzzing when he came back into the restaurant. He was talking about all the things they had in common. That's when he told me he'd arranged to finish his shift early so he could be her date for the rest of the evening. I was thrilled, but after everything she'd been through, I just said, 'Don't mess this up.' Sam thought he was punching above his weight, and I know he had a quiet word with himself as he changed out of his uniform. Even so, I knew he'd do fine just being himself. Talk to Sam for two minutes and chances are you'll fall in love.

> ❜ *Whatever happens, a date can be a learning experience and a chance to build some confidence.* ❜

It's easy to dismiss anyone who fails to show up for a date. For sure, it's a terrible thing to leave anyone waiting without some kind of explanation. At the same time there are many reasons why someone might not have the courage to see it through, and it would be wrong to leap to conclusions. This could be their first date in ten years, and nerves have got the better of them, or they could be coming out of a painful divorce. My advice to anyone in that situation is to reach out to the people who care for you. Whether it's a friend or family member, let them know you're wobbling, and give them a chance to steer you back on course. Often it's just a case of being reminded of all the good things about yourself that others like and admire, but it might be enough to get you through the restaurant doors – and from there you'll never look back.

Whatever happens, a date can be a learning experience and a chance to build some confidence. But if you can't go through with it, always be sure to notify your date. It's the decent thing to do, and though it might cause upset they'll have to respect the fact that you were honest with them. Should you be the one left waiting, don't lose sight of the fact that it says nothing about you. It also frees you up to enjoy time with someone with the potential to make a genuine connection.

UP CLOSE & PERSONAL

BETTER LATE THAN NEVER
GUS & JO

With beauty, poise and wisdom on her side, this 43-year-old divorcée knows exactly what she's hoping to find on her date with destiny at the restaurant. On a basic level, an actual date would be nice. When Fred breaks the news that Gus has been delayed, Jo handles the situation with grace. While some might pretend to look busy on their phones, she coolly slots in her earplugs and tunes out to music. When Gus finally shows up, Jo greets him with a scowl, asks, 'Where the hell have you been?' and makes out she's been waiting for several hours. Just as her delayed date wonders if he should've turned around at the entrance, Jo drops the act and switches to a disarming smile.

PART ONE
GEORGIA & . . .

Gorgeous Georgia could turn anyone's eye. Sadly, her date doesn't know what he's missing out on when he fails to show up. 'I think he got cold feet,' offers Fred, who has to break the news. 'He's missing out,' he reasons, and spreads his hands wide. Georgia struggles to maintain her composure, and drowns her sorrows in another drink at the bar. There, as she shares her bad news on the phone to a friend, Alex walks in to await a date that won't go well, and the pair exchange a friendly glance . . .

CLOSE CALL
TOMMY & ADAM

After several years alone, Tommy, 23, is still looking for Mr Right. But with one attempt at finding love in the *First Dates* restaurant already under his belt, his confidence is fragile. The first to arrive at the bar, Tommy orders a drink and then keeps one eye anxiously on the door.

Every time it opens he prepares himself for the worst. 'I've been here, like, an hour,' he complains on the phone to his mum. 'Alright, maybe ten minutes.' The poor guy is so convinced he's been stood up that when Adam does show up he practically floats off the stool with relief. As things turn out, the date doesn't prove to be a perfect match, but at least Tommy can say that he made it as far as the table.

WHATEVER
MULA & . . .

'Imagine if it's real love,' bubbles South London hairdresser Mula, before heading into the restaurant to find out if Cupid's looked kindly upon her. As time at the bar ticks by, measured by mojitos, our solo girl begins to wonder if everyone's treasured cherub is on a day off. The harsh fact is each man who walks through the door is here for someone else. When the news filters through that her date's had cold feet, poor Mula finds solace on the bench outside with a complimentary bowl of chips. 'Thank you, bitch, for wasting my time,' she mutters into the cool night air.

'I could've been doing, like, whatever . . .'

❧ AND FINALLY ❧

In life we will always have difficult times. It is how we get up again that matters. If we clear out the people who aren't right for us from our lives, we can make space for the ones who are.

Setting out on a date is like climbing on to a stage. It is easy to feel as if everyone is watching you; and that can be intense, should you find yourself alone under the spotlight. It also takes courage to put yourself up there. You must remind yourself of this, should your date fail to join you. So hold your head up high. Their absence says everything about them and nothing about you.

Ultimately, love is rarely straightforward. Even so, we cannot allow disappointments to stop us from being happy. If anything, let them be the thing that spurs you on to finding someone incredible. There is a soulmate out there for you.

"
Love all,
trust a few,
do wrong to none.

"

WILLIAM SHAKESPEARE

ALL'S WELL THAT ENDS WELL

LAURA

FROM:

Staines

BEST DATE EVER:

I've never been on one in my life. My boyfriend started out as my best friend.

WORST DATE EVER:

Doesn't apply.

FIRST KISS:

Behind the bus shelter, age 12.

CRUSH:

Benedict Cumberbatch

PERFECT ROMANTIC NIGHT OUT:

Anything outdoors, like a picnic with wine (one bottle limit), food and lots of chat.

PERFECT ROMANTIC NIGHT IN:

It has to involve sweets – preferably a whole tub. Some alcohol and *First Dates* on the TV.

GO-TO DATE OUTFIT:

I'm influenced by the girls I work with in the restaurant. If they're wearing something nice I ask myself if it would work for me, too. As a result, my favourite outfit is all down to my colleagues – a long skirt with a little strappy top and heels.

EVER HAD A MISHAP AT THE RESTAURANT?

I picked up a knife at a couple's table and dropped it on their wine glass. Not only that, it smashed the glass, which spilled wine everywhere. Awful.

FAVOURITE *FIRST DATES* COUPLE:

I just loved Naomi and Jo. They were so perfect for each other.

FUNNIEST *FIRST DATES* MOMENT:

It would have to be when Sav came under fire from his first date, Cat, for daring to wear a turtleneck. The poor guy!

WHAT HAS WORKING ON *FIRST DATES* TAUGHT YOU ABOUT LOVE?

So much. It's just been one huge introduction to the dating world. The best things are the dating tips, like what to wear and what to say. I've also learned a lot about all the different elements that go into making the perfect date.

WHY SHOULD PEOPLE GO ON *FIRST DATES*?

We make every effort to bring people together who might just work as a couple. We consider everything we possibly can, and so there's a good chance that if you walk through the restaurant door you'll find the date of your dreams.

We make every effort to bring people together who might just work as a couple.

Just Friends

Chapter Sixteen

A DIFFERENT KIND OF LOVE

I cannot see a problem with two people remaining friends after a date. After all, you don't have to sleep with everybody you meet. But make sure the friendship is a mutual one and you haven't confused it with something else.

If you are hoping that maybe one day the friendship will lead to a relationship, you are on shaky ground. You should never go into a friendship hoping for that.

> *Make sure the friendship is a mutual one and you haven't confused it with something else.*

There was this one girl I used to date years ago; it didn't work out. She's nice, but for months after we had broken up I would get three or four texts a day from her. She even used to buy me presents. As terrible as it may sound, I wished she would stop because I felt guilty that she was still carrying a torch for me.

When we met up I had nothing to say to her; I only saw her because I felt like I should (and she is very sweet). But I was so busy all the time that it felt like I was just going through the motions. And I suspect the only reason she wanted to be friends with me was because she was still hoping that one day we'd be together like we once were.

If you do want to stay friends with someone after a date or a relationship then it has to be very 'clean'. I cannot be sure this girl still likes me, but she certainly acts like she does, and so I wonder if I am being unfair being friends with her.

Is there such a thing as too many friends? That is up to you. But if someone is going to add something to your life then that is a friend. If you are going to be avoiding phone calls and text messages from someone all the time, you clearly do not want them in your life.

Friends with benefits is a very common thing these days. If you can be happy sleeping with someone with no commitment, that is fine. But if you think you may fall for someone eventually, when you know they don't feel the same, you must steer clear. No good can come of it.

Lisa and Terry have managed to make it work as friends. They were not ever going to be a couple, but the fact that they help each other out if they need a 'plus one' or they can act as a wingman (or wingwoman) is wonderful. Neither of them is expecting anything else from the other one, and they both know where they stand, so that friendship works perfectly.

You must both be on the same page and not have any ulterior motive for a friendship to last. It can happen, even if you first met on a date. I have seen it work out many times.

HOW WAS IT FOR YOU?

LISA

'If it doesn't work out with someone, why not stay in touch? They may have a mate you fancy.'

Not every meal in the *First Dates* restaurant can lead to romance, but you could end up making a friend instead. Although 47-year-old Lisa knew Terry wasn't the man for her, the pair have managed to stay friends and still meet up for nights out. 'I applied for the show because I thought it would be a crack,' explains Lisa. 'I thought, "Nothing ventured, nothing gained." I went on the day with the attitude that even if the guy I was set up with was a monster with two heads I was going to have a good time.'

Jeweller Lisa knew from the word go she and Terry weren't a match made in heaven, but she was still determined to have a fun night. 'The minute I looked at Terry, I knew he wasn't for me. When you meet someone you've got to at least fancy them, and I just didn't get that feeling of excitement you get when you "know". It didn't help that Terry forgot my name pretty much straight away. He was trying to guess it for about half an hour and kept getting it wrong. I must admit, I'd forgotten his as well, but I blagged my way through until someone else said it, and then I was off the hook. You can only get away with calling someone "treacle" or "hun" for so long. I was a bit gutted, because I'd bought a new outfit and had my hair done especially, but you can't win them all.'

To make sure there were clear boundaries when it came to settling the bill for their meal Lisa insisted she and Terry both paid their way. 'We went Dutch and I thought if we did that there wouldn't be any confusion. If you let someone pay for you, you owe them something. We had a nice meal and some good banter, but at the end of the evening I was honest and I said, "Look, you're a lovely fella, Tel, but you're not what I'm looking for." He turned around and said, "You're ninety per cent what I wanted." And all I could think was, "And ten per cent what you didn't?" I wasn't offended at all. He was so out of the dating game that the comment just made me laugh.'

> ❛ *You get to an age where you don't want to play games any more.* ❜

But that wasn't the end of the story. Rather than going their separate ways, Lisa and Terry went for a drink after dinner. 'We only went as mates but we did get on well. I liked his company and he was a good laugh, but there was still no attraction from my end and I didn't want to rip his clothes off. There was never going to be any romance between us but we clearly liked each other as friends, so we agreed to stay in touch. The next day Tel phoned me and said he'd had a really nice time. We've carried on texting ever since.'

The pair became such good mates they went to a party together a few weeks later. 'I stayed open-minded about things but I also made it very clear that we were just going as friends and he was fine with that. We had a laugh together but we both knew it wasn't going to blossom into anything – now or in the future. You get to an age where you don't want to play games any more, and you would rather save time by being upfront about things. I didn't feel bad telling Terry I didn't fancy him, because it was a much nicer thing to do than pretending we may fall in love at some point. I went on a date with a guy once and we knew as soon as we met each other it was obvious it wasn't going to happen. We sat in the beer garden of a pub having awkward silences and then he went to the toilet and didn't come back. I was so upset. At least I was upfront with Terry. Doing a runner is a terrible thing to do to someone. The guy texted 'sorry' afterwards but the fact he didn't have the guts to be honest made my blood boil. You should always treat people how you want to be treated.'

Lisa, who is currently single, reckons it's a good idea to stay friends with exes – because you never know when they'll come in handy. 'Terry and I still message each other to see how the other one is and have a little chat, and we'll definitely see each other again. Sometimes I go on dates with blokes and I think, "I don't fancy you, and I don't even want to be mates. I've got enough mates." But I didn't with Terry, because we've got a similar sense of humour and I did like him as a person. I've stayed friends with quite a lot of guys I've been out with or been on dates with. It's always good if you need a "plus one" for something. It's gutting if you like someone and it doesn't work out, but there's no reason why you can't stay in touch if they haven't done you any harm. And at the end of the day, even if it didn't work out with them, they may have a mate you fancy.'

CICI SAYS

Lisa was full of such energy and bubbles. As soon as I saw her waiting for her date, I wanted to sit down at her table and have a good chat. I was really hoping she'd find love at the restaurant, because she looked like someone with so much to offer. When Terry arrived, he seemed like a sweet, kind and decent man. You could see that in his eyes, in many ways.

At the same time, that transparency meant Terry couldn't hide the fact that he was holding on to something. Lisa certainly registered this early on. Even I could tell that someone in his past still meant a great deal to him. Then he started talking about his ex. People say this isn't something you should do on a date, but I disagree. That person has played an important part in your life, after all. What matters is whether you've moved on. In Terry's case, however, it seemed to me that his ex was still special to him. There was still a lot of love there, and it was heartbreaking when he took himself off to the loo for a quiet weep. As a result, even though it seemed like Lisa liked him, it was never going to be anything more than a friendship situation.

It's easy to think that coming away from a date as genuine friends is some kind of failure, but that's not the case at all. It's very different from being friend-zoned, when often that's just a polite way of saying you're unlikely to see each other again. It comes down to honesty. Even though romance wasn't on the cards for Lisa and Terry, it was evident that they genuinely recognized how much they had in common – and that's something to be valued. I know this from personal experience. A guy once said to me, 'Whatever happens on this date, I want to be your friend.' I took that quite negatively at first, thinking he was giving me the brush-off, but once I realized he was being absolutely heartfelt it became a positive thing.

In every way, I consider Terry and Lisa's date to be a success. Why? Because they each found a friend. That's a precious thing. You just have to be clear with one another if that's where it's heading, because this is a friendship that's sprung from a potentially romantic situation. Of course, sometimes a relationship can grow over time. In this situation, you both need to review how things are going to avoid mixed messages or causing confusion. It all comes down to honesty, and the fact that at the very least a good friendship is something to be treasured.

> ❛ *It's easy to think that coming away from a date as genuine friends is some kind of failure, but that's not the case at all.* ❜

UP CLOSE & PERSONAL

BEST DATE FRIENDS FOR EVER
DEBBIE & ANN

In her own words, twice-married A&E receptionist Debbie is 'in the infancy of lesbianism'. She's cautious but keen to meet women and see how things go. On paper, divorcée Ann looks like the perfect match. Ann

certainly seems to think so as the evening progresses, and even holds out hope at the end that Debbie feels the same way. Her nerves come out in force as she awaits her date's response, and though it isn't as she hoped, the offer of friendship is undeniably genuine and sealed with a heartfelt hug.

KID-ZONED
PAUL & VERONA

Over dinner, make-up artist and mum Verona begins to feel the heat with firefighter Paul. He's charming, handsome, and the conversation flows as she talks about life as a parent. 'The date went well,' she says afterwards, flushed with excitement at meeting a match. A moment later, Paul takes the hot seat beside her and suggests that perhaps they should settle for friends. 'If I had the choice,' he admits among other things, 'I'd rather see someone who didn't have kids.' As the taxi departs to take her home, Verona is faced with questions about the date from her driver. 'He totally dissed me,' she says.

PRETEND FRIENDS
STEPHAN & NIKE

Performance art student Stephan has a big heart and is immediately attracted to his date. PE teacher Nike is tired of being 'always the bridesmaid' and is looking out for 'the One'. Sadly, Stephan doesn't qualify. He overflows with confidence and energy but it's all a bit intense for Nike. 'I think there's more of a friendship here,' she tells him diplomatically, but there's no hiding the truth, and relations cool considerably. 'It's been a wicked experience,' she adds later, before deciding to just spell it out. 'But we will not be in contact.'

DATING DIRECT
WILL & LOUISA

Ex-public schoolgirl Louisa, 20, is still learning when it comes to men. All she can do is be herself, she decides, so her blind date finds her as she was 'when she popped out of the uterus'. Supermarket manager Will, 26, is certainly disarmed by Louisa's dry humour and direct approach, and struggles to respond on returning from a restroom break. 'Was the loo OK?' she inquires. 'Successful?' Later, Will is quick to speak up when it comes to the issue of whether they'll see each other again. 'In a friendly way,' he says, 'but perhaps not in a dating way.'

❧ AND FINALLY ❧

Sometimes we place a great deal of hope and expectation on a date. Naturally we all want to meet someone special and for love to blossom, but often it just is not meant to play out that way. Instead, we might see the potential for a firm friendship, and this is something to be celebrated. It is simply a different kind of love, but one that should be equally cherished.

While making a friend from a date can be truly amazing, staying close to an ex is a very special thing. After all, the fact you liked each other was the reason you got together in the first place. But there should never be an expectation that romance will return between you. Otherwise the friendship can no longer continue as it is.

"

Friendship always benefits; love sometimes injures.

"

SENECA

Second Dates

Chapter Seventeen

❧ STRANGERS NO MORE ❧

Some people get more nervous on second dates because of the anticipation and excitement. Alternatively, they worry that it won't go as well as they want it to. While first dates are usually fun and light, the second date is often more serious because it involves a deeper level of intimacy.

Someone may be able to laugh and joke their way through a first date but a second date is when you start to show someone who you truly are. It is when you get to ask some of the more revealing questions you wanted to ask on the first date. You can delve a little deeper and reveal more of yourself, too.

> *The second date is often more serious because it involves a deeper level of intimacy.*

So many scary thoughts can go through your head. What if they like the first-date version of you better? What if they prefer that person who was drunker and louder? Or what if they were drawn to you because you were quieter than usual because you were nervous?

If you go on a second date it means you actually like someone, and that is where things change. If a second date goes well, you know you are on to something good and that you weren't simply swept up in the moment when you first met.

I would suggest doing something fun and different for your second date. I love the fact that Naomi and Jo went go-karting. I bet they learned so much about each other that day, and had a great time doing it. Unusual dates can be the most revealing.

I love it when I hear that people who have met in the *First Dates* restaurant are going on second dates. Sometimes they work and sometimes they don't, but at least they are being bold enough to try. Dating is all good experience. I have said it before, and I will say it again: building confidence takes practice.

We can condition our minds. If you want to be a basketball player or an Olympic athlete you need to practise every day and stay focused, and you need to do the same when you want to find love. If you want to meet someone to spend your life with you can't sit back and wait for them to come to you. You have to explore your heart and take a gamble on romance.

Should you go on a second date if you're not one hundred per cent sure about someone? Of course! How will you know if you do not try? All you will lose is one night of your life . . . but you could very well find love.

⟋⟍ HOW WAS IT FOR YOU? ⟋⟍

NAOMI

JO

'Our second date was perfect because that's when everything clicked into place.'

Before they both decided to enter the world of *First Dates*, nanny Jo had been single for two years, while personal trainer Naomi had been flying solo for six months. Fast-forward and the couple are now living very happily together with Naomi's cat, Lucy.

'I just thought I'd give *First Dates* a go and see what it was like, and maybe get a friend out of it. Or at least have a nice meal. Now I've ended up with a girlfriend,' begins Naomi.

'I was nervous because I thought I was going to make a fool out of myself or get set up with a butch lesbian,' continues 27-year-old Jo. 'I was so happy when I saw Naomi. I thought straight away, "They've done a good job there." I had figured they'd probably just find some random girl on the street and plonk us together but they matched us really well. There wasn't a massive spark straight away, and we didn't hugely fancy each other, but we got on so that was a very good place to start. It's funny because viewers could tell there was chemistry, but we didn't feel it until later on.'

SECOND DATES

The girls were soon swapping stories and, as Naomi explains, they both felt like there could be something between them. 'We talked about everything, from our jobs to our families to what TV we like to watch. We asked a lot of typical dating questions, and although we were having a bit of banter it still felt strange because it's not every day you go on a blind date. Jo made me laugh, which is always a good thing, and I definitely wanted to go for a drink with her afterwards.'

Jo was on the same wavelength as Naomi and decided that if she paid for dinner, Naomi would have no choice but to buy her a drink by way of a thank you. 'I did my best to pay but Naomi wasn't having any of it. So we ended up splitting the bill – and then went for a drink anyway,' laughs Jo. 'Even though we weren't falling madly in love with each other, neither of us wanted the night to end. So we got a rickshaw into Soho and carried on the date in a bar.'

'We had a couple of drinks and I built up the courage and asked her if I could kiss her,' blushes 23-year-old Naomi. 'Seriously, who asks for permission to kiss someone? But it did the job and we had our first smooch. We both said there and then we'd like to see each other again. We went our separate ways that night but we texted each other until late and we spoke on the phone for about three hours the next day.'

The girls speedily arranged their second date at a go-karting track in Croydon. 'I drove from London to Naomi's house and I was sat outside her house on the phone to my friend saying, "Should I kiss her hello? How does this work? What should I do?"' smiles Jo. 'Then Naomi walked over to my car and kissed me on the lips and I was, like, "Yes!" I was only going to stay for one night but we had such a good time I ended up staying for the whole weekend and meeting her friends and everything. Thankfully they were all great – and thank God I got on with them, because Naomi told me later that if I hadn't got on with them it would have been a problem.'

That second date (or rather, weekend) was the start of something beautiful, and after spending six months meeting up every weekend the couple decided to move in together. 'I moved house and I was going to get a flatmate, but I didn't know how I'd find anyone who would understand me or put up with my mess,' admits Naomi. 'I kept hinting to Jo, and eventually the penny dropped and she said, "Are you asking me to move in with you?" and I was, like, "Yep." I hadn't exactly been subtle, but because we hadn't been together that long I don't think she was expecting it.'

They share a home in Surrey and they would recommend having a second 'just in case' date to anyone. Because you never know what could happen. 'If you're umming and ahhing about someone and you don't go on a second date, you'll never know,' says Jo. 'You've got to give someone a chance. Even though there weren't sparks initially, we got on well and I wanted to give it more time and see how it went. And I'm so pleased I did. Our second date was perfect because that's when everything clicked into place.'

And Naomi couldn't agree more. 'On a second date you can relax and be yourself more. On our first date I kept worrying about whether my lipstick was smudged and I was more aware of what I was saying, but when you meet again it feels easier somehow. You can just enjoy your time with them. Or not, in which case you don't see them again. You could be missing out on someone amazing if you don't give it a go. If we'd gone our separate ways straight after dinner we wouldn't ever have seen each other again, and then none of this would have happened.'

❛ You've got to give someone a chance. ❜

LAURA SAYS

You could say Naomi and Jo were well matched because they were both such pretty girls, but there was so much more about them that guaranteed they'd be seeing each other again.

On a blind date, most couples take a few minutes to find a way into a conversation. When Jo met Naomi at the bar, they related to each other more like old friends with lots of catching up ahead of them. It was amazing to watch. No awkward pauses, no dramas or disasters. Just two perfectly suited young women chatting and smiling and looking totally relaxed in each other's company. Even when Jo admitted that this was her first same-sex date, having previously been out with men, Naomi held her gaze as if assessing whether or not she was here with serious intentions, and then just went with her gut feeling. Watching them get to know each other over dinner that evening, we all knew it was the right move to make.

> ❛ *It's easy to get hung up about how much time should pass before arranging a second date . . . I think if you're keen then just sort it out.* ❜

The great thing about meeting a stranger in the *First Dates* restaurant is that you'll always leave knowing exactly where you stand. I love that moment when couples are asked the question directly: Will you be seeing each other again? OK, it's awkward, but let's face it, everyone wants to know – not least the two people in the hot seat. And with the answer out in the open, it means they can leave without any uncertainty in their minds. That's so great. It's what makes our restaurant so unique.

When Jo and Naomi were asked if a second date was on the cards, it was totally obvious how they'd both respond. It wasn't just their body language, beaming smiles, or the fact that they clearly didn't want the date to finish. It was the way their conversation had changed towards the end of the meal. How? They started making plans. Loads of couples do this if things are working out well. So, over dessert you might hear one person say something like, 'I'm in a band, and when you come to see me play . . .' Or, 'My mum is going to love you . . .' It's a subconscious way of setting up a chance to see more of each other, and if the other person reacts positively then chances are they'll finish by swapping numbers. It doesn't guarantee a lifelong romance, but it's a great chance to see if things will develop.

It's easy to get hung up about how much time should pass before arranging a second date. Personally, I think if you're keen then just sort it out. If you call but they don't pick up, my advice is leave a message rather than hanging up and trying again. They might just be busy, after all. But if you don't hear back then focus on moving on, and fast. If anything, it says more about their inability to be open and honest than it does about you. Then you can chalk up that first date as practice for the one that leads to a second date and beyond.

UP CLOSE & PERSONAL

SMELL THE LUST
JAYDEN & ISABEL

The date's gone well for 19-year-old childminder Isabel, and Jayden, 26. They have plenty in common, from a fluency in Spanish to a mutual friend. Even though said friend has a reputation as a player, and happens to be Jayden's best mate, the couple get through the date in one piece. It's clear that Jayden would like to see more of Isabel, but does she agree? 'I can literally smell the lust on him,' she laughs. While making it quite clear she's not a 'one-night-stand kind of girl', and despite his infamous wingman back home, she still agrees to see him again. Jayden can't believe his luck. 'You are quite adorable,' he says as they head for the taxi rank together.

FEED ME
BEN & HOLLY

Fitness enthusiast and calorie counter Ben, 29, has struck lucky with 23-year-old Holly. They're a perfect match in many ways, though Ben's blind date has taken to tempting him with something he's struggling to resist. 'Go on,' purrs Holly, waving a spoonful of dessert in front of his mouth. Once Ben gives in the couple take turns to feed each other, and before we know it the plate is empty. Leaving the restaurant arm in arm, Ben realizes he'll need to make some changes to his evening. 'I was planning on going for a run,' he says, 'but I didn't realize I'd be dating someone who'd be feeding me carbs.'

THE GREATEST DATE
SASHA & AARON

'That was great,' says customer service adviser Sasha, with a dreamy look in her eyes. 'You were great,' she adds, and turns to her blind date. 'Was I?' asks part-time model Aaron, flattered beyond measure. 'Yeah, you were.' Sasha cannot stop smiling about their time in the restaurant. 'And you smell great!' For a girl with a history of going out with 'arseholes' she can't believe that Cupid has saved her from a lonely existence 'with twenty-seven cats'. Afterwards, this made-for-each-other couple climb into the same cab, where Sasha bellows, 'Elephant and Castle, honey!' and prepares to continue their night.

CAN'T CHANGE ME
GARY & ELLIS

Ellis, 47, is a disco-loving personal trainer. Over dinner, in the company of dashing blind date Gary, his eyes begin to sparkle like glitter balls. Gary is great company, with a touching life story that draws Ellis into his orbit. The couple have a lot in common, apart from the fact that Ellis is teetotal and Gary doesn't understand how anyone can have a good time without a glass in their hand. Patiently, Ellis explains that it's just not his thing, but Gary refuses to admit defeat. 'Give me your number,' he persists on the street outside. 'We'll go out and have a drink.'

AND FINALLY

What is life without risk? If a second date is not successful
at least you know you were courageous enough to find out.
Ultimately, you will have lost very little. And conversely, it could
be the beginning of something unbelievable that changes things
for ever. But here's the thing – you won't find out unless you try.

We can never truly get to know someone on a first date. We
might fall for them on a superficial level and see something in
their eyes that makes us want to learn more about them, but
only time will reveal what makes them tick. A second date
might take you one step closer to that discovery, or open
your eyes to the fact that you're not right for each other. It is
a journey, after all. One that begins from the moment you set
eyes on each other and has the potential to last a lifetime.

"

Good night, good night!
Parting is such sweet
sorrow, that I shall
say good night till
it be morrow.

"

WILLIAM SHAKESPEARE
ROMEO AND JULIET

DATE LINES . . .

THE SAID WHAT?

Find out who's behind these quotes
on page 251

22. 'Why wouldn't you split it [the bill]? Because you're a woman'

23. 'Life's too short. One shot. Enjoy every minute'

24. 'I'd go on another date with you, babe'
    'Yes! Get in!'

25. 'I occasionally cross-dress'

26. 'Can I go on another date?'

27. 'I've told people about the girl at the bar. Obviously told them she's pretty decent. Probably out of my league to be fair'

28. 'Basically, I have a tattoo of a black cock on my toe'
    'On your what?'

29. 'I don't want a girl who doesn't want me to be happy with who I am'

30. 'This time around I am hoping for someone a bit more like me'

31. 'I feel really excited. I've got a really warm, glowing feeling all of a sudden'

32. 'I would, I think, be up for a second date'
    'Maybe somewhere like Nandos?'

Back for More

♥

Chapter Eighteen

THE SEARCH CONTINUES

Love is not always a straight and easy road, but every twist and turn will help you get to where you want to be. If you falter in your search for romance pull yourself up and try, try, try again. It is said that nothing worth having comes easily, and that is often true of love.

You need determination and resilience to go out and get what you want. I've never stayed down for too long after heartbreak. It is important to take ownership if relationships don't work. You have to have closure when a relationship finishes and move on, or you will stay feeling stuck for ever.

> *Love is not always a straight and easy road, but every twist and turn will help you get to where you want to be.*

If a date doesn't work out, remember that you can come back stronger afterwards, having learned something from it. It doesn't say anything about who you are just because you weren't right for someone. So as soon as you leave that date, let it go.

That is why serial daters are always seeing someone new; because they bounce back quickly from disappointments and they are always open to the right person coming along. They don't close themselves off when they are wounded, they let someone else in. I'm not saying that everyone has to go out and date many people, but you may have to try on many suits before you find the one that fits you best. So why not try out different styles?

I don't believe love becomes harder when you get older. I won't accept that excuse from anyone. It can be whatever you want it to be at whatever age you are. My dad always says to me, 'We are not meant to live in isolation. We are meant to live with people.' And even if you're elderly or widowed or divorced, you make a choice about whether or not you want to stay in and be on your own, or go out and meet people in the same position as you.

Sometimes older people lose confidence and think no one will want to date them because they are of a certain age. But there are many people of all ages who are looking to meet someone. I don't think there is any difference between older and younger people dating. It is no easier or harder.

Trust and faith are incredibly important in love. You have to know with every fibre of your being that you are capable of meeting someone. As soon as doubt sets in, you are setting yourself up for failure. If you start to have negative thoughts, you have to work hard to stop them or they can grow.

We are all the masters of our own destiny and if you want to find the person who is right for you there is nothing stopping you except your own mind. And remember, it is your mind, so you can change it if you wish.

Love is out there for each one of us. We just have to keep remembering how much we deserve it.

HOW WAS IT FOR YOU?

꧁ **LUKE** ꧂

'I felt like I'd lost to Rocky twice ... I was desperate to get back in the ring.'

When you walk through the doors of the *First Dates* restaurant, it's only natural to bring high hopes. You're here to find love, after all. While some find their soulmates across the candlelit table, others aren't so fortunate. For 23-year-old supermarket worker Luke, it didn't just take two visits before he struck lucky. Our man with the prolific ginger beard – and one of the most memorable lines ever spluttered over dinner – soldiered through three dates before Cupid's arrow struck.

'I hadn't really been on dates before,' explains this engaging young Londoner with puppy-like charm. 'So when I met Nicky on my first visit I dressed smart and went in with loads of confidence. I thought I'd tell a couple of jokes, make her laugh and she'd be all over me. When I'm out in clubs, in a crowded environment, that side of things has never been an issue,' he explains. 'Then I found myself sitting down on a one to one, trying to sell myself to a stranger, and reality hit hard.'

Looking back, Luke knows precisely when things went wrong on that first date. Even now, it's enough to make him cringe. 'I told her I liked a bit of "Netflix and chill", and her face just dropped. It was meant as a joke,' he insists, 'and I tried to bring it back by pretending I didn't know what it meant, but even then I knew I'd messed up big time.'

While a nation laughed, Luke spent the rest of his date resigned to the fact that their evening would end in separate taxis. 'Nicky put me in my place,' he freely admits. 'I'm used to girls laughing along with me, and suddenly I was in a very different situation. She was looking for someone serious, and here was this young lad making crude suggestions across the table. It made me realize my confidence wasn't as rock steady as I had thought.' While most people in his position would've headed for home with no plans to face the world again, Luke left with the conviction that he could learn from the experience. 'I was speaking without thinking,' he says. 'I also realized that I hadn't listened enough, and just came away with a sense that I could've done better.'

Luke didn't just return to the restaurant with a fresh pair of ears. On meeting Shannon, he'd chosen to ditch the velvet jacket for a T-shirt, jeans and trainers. 'I just hadn't felt comfortable the first time,' he explains, 'but I think I took the dressing down too far. I looked like I'd shown up for an evening round my mate's house with the PlayStation. I was a hot mess.'

Luke attributes his apparent lack of effort to the fact that he found himself almost instantaneously friend-zoned. 'The conversation died down quickly,' he says. 'Shannon was gorgeous, but the click just wasn't there. My confidence was already low after my first date, and I just kind of gave up on it. I went in as a listener, but ended up being just too quiet.' As a result, when Shannon expressed an interest in maybe staying in touch but nothing more, Luke responded with the resignation of a man who had read her mind over starters.

'I felt like I'd lost to Rocky twice,' he says, reflecting on the lowest moment of his experience in the *First Dates* restaurant. 'I was pretty down about it for a while, but then I started thinking I had something to prove to myself, big time. I even started saying to my mates, "Boys, I'm telling you, if I can go back in I will kill it!" I was desperate to get back in the ring.'

Before his final return, Luke tried out online dating a couple of times, and it's here he feels that he finally found his form. 'Things went well, and that's when I realized that my first two visits to the restaurant hadn't been a waste of time. I'd learned loads, so when I went back and met Hannah I knew just how to handle the evening.' With a trimmed beard, dressing comfortably but not too casually, and tooled up with champagne and flowers, Luke unleashed his inner romantic. 'I was completely at ease with the conversation,' he says proudly. 'I threw in some jokes, but nothing that would kill the evening, and made sure I paid the right compliments. Making her laugh was still important to me,' he says, 'but I also wanted her to feel like she was with a gent.'

Afterwards, Luke seemed genuinely surprised when Hannah expressed an interest in seeing him again. 'I'd been pied twice,' he says, 'so I was ready for the worst. I thought she'd say I was a cuddly bear kind of friend, but it turned out so much better. I was legit buzzing when she said she wanted to see me again.'

So, after three valiant attempts at finding love, did Luke find 'the One'? Luke reflects, and for once doesn't blame himself. 'We don't live close to each other,' he says, 'and our work schedules kept getting in the way whenever we tried to arrange meeting up. It was just one of those things. Hannah's a lovely girl, and I wish her well, but I'm back in the game,' he admits, and with no regrets whatsoever. 'I don't want to sound big-headed,' he chuckles, 'but I'm just so confident now. It's a joke! I'm still trying to perfect how I present myself, but nowadays I can get a second date with ease.' If anything, he says, such a public learning experience helps girls to understand that he's a trier with a good heart. Even when he's reminded of his 'Netflix and chill' moment, Luke holds his head high. 'Though it can be a bit awkward when people yell it at me across the street and I'm with my mum,' he points out.

For a young man who has chalked up more visits than most to the restaurant, what advice does Luke have for those new to the dating game? 'Aim to please while being yourself, and never give up,' he says simply. 'Even if you fall off the horse, get back on it as soon as you can.'

❛ *I was legit buzzing when she said she wanted to see me again.* ❜

CICI SAYS

Luke is such a funny guy, and you can't help but laugh in his company. As soon as I met him, I thought, 'You're a winner.' The strange thing is that it wasn't until the end of his second date that I realized how nervous he was. Outwardly, he creates the impression of being a young guy who understands himself and knows what he wants in life. It's like he uses comedy as a cover, and in a sense that made me love him all the more.

I was genuinely shocked when Luke's first date didn't go well. Then again, I was serving at another table when he had his 'Netflix and chill' moment. He went too far with that, for sure. It's funny, but maybe not on a first date.

It meant Nicky suddenly saw him as a kid, not a man. She wanted to see a potential boyfriend, but instead she saw a boy. Many guys in his situation would've regarded the evening as a mistake. Luke didn't do that, and when he returned for a second attempt I was seriously rooting for him.

Even though he entered the friend-zone on that date, I rated Luke for taking a different approach. He'd realized that talking to a girl in a restaurant is very different from chatting up someone in a club. OK, so he might've done a little too much listening, which made it hard for Shannon to see anything more than a nice guy, but it was worth a shot. That Luke took it on the chin and came back for a third crack left me with nothing but admiration. It might've taken him a few attempts, but when he delivered it came from the heart.

Luke's experience reminded me that every date we ever go on is a learning opportunity. Even if things don't work out, you can always take away a valuable lesson. The key is not to beat yourself up about it. Instead, analyse what went wrong and be constructive in working out if you need to make changes to your dating approach. Then there are other times when you do everything right but there's simply no spark.

Of course it can be tough if you have a knock-back, but we can all take a leaf out of Luke's book and refuse to give in. If I'm ever at a low point, I turn to friends and let them help remind me that the dating game is something to be enjoyed, no matter what the outcome.

UP CLOSE & PERSONAL

MR CHEDDAR
TERRY & LAUREN

On a previous visit to the restaurant, Essex DJ Terry 'Turbo' admitted to sleeping with hundreds of women. Now, waiting for his next date, he's worried this admission might mean his reputation precedes him. 'If he starts,' Lauren warns beforehand, 'he's messing with the wrong girl.' Sure enough, Terry is on fine form when he looks her in the eyes and tells her that she's beautiful. Lauren rolls her eyes. 'Cheesy,' she says. 'Mr Cheddar.' Sure enough, Terry fails to recover, and though the date might end in different taxis, we can be sure this lovable player isn't out of the game.

#PAOLOBULOUS
PAOLO & MARIO

Paolo's first date stumbled when he revealed a penchant for wearing stilettos. Now he's back but unrepentant. 'I'm still the same person,' he insists. 'Just a lot taller.' In many ways, the experience has strengthened Paolo's resolve to meet someone who accepts him as he is, and there's no better man to do that than Mario. When Paolo seizes the moment to show a picture of his cross-dressing alter ego, tagged 'PAOLOBULOUS', Mario is nothing less than impressed. 'I'm so excited to hear about this,' he says, as Paolo's tentative steps back into the dating game get into a strut and then a stride.

MUM'S THE WORD
CORINNE & WILL

The nation's rooting for Corinne, who'd been left in tears after her last date at the restaurant. 'I wasn't expecting a boyfriend,' she sniffs, 'but I was expecting a guy to actually like me.' Bravely, she's back again and facing property developer Will. Tongues are tied to begin with, but then the conversation turns to tattoos, and Corinne reveals she has a Playboy bunny on her bum. On common ground at last, Will tells her that he has special letters inked on a very precious part of his anatomy. 'Shut the front door!' shrieks Corinne as the penny drops. 'Really?' While she may not be sure how to handle this – in every sense, no doubt – it brings the couple together for a date they'll both remember.

PART TWO
GEORGIA & . . . ALEX

Having been stood up on her first visit, and still stung by the experience, Georgia arrives for another attempt at finding love. She's back at the bar, awaiting her date, and her face is a picture when a familiar figure walks in. As for Alex, his eyes light up on seeing 'the one that got away' from his last time in the restaurant, when he met Georgia briefly ahead of a date that didn't work out for him. This time the couple sense that fate has looked upon them kindly and they make the most of a memorable date.

❧ **AND FINALLY** ❧

Whether we are gay, straight, bisexual or asexual, ultimately we all want to find love and be happy. It is the Holy Grail. There are no rights or wrongs – or hard and fast rules – when it comes to matters of the heart. Sometimes your heart knows a lot more than you do, so be sure to listen to it.

As a subject love is as important as mathematics or chemistry, but it cannot be taught. We seek our lessons from experience, and gain insight from our failures as much as our successes. Yes, it is tempting to give up when we are feeling wounded, but those who pick themselves up and return to the fray are heroes in my book. And when victory comes, it is well deserved.

"

*Experience is the
teacher of all things.*

"

JULIUS CAESAR

ACKNOWLEDGEMENTS

It takes more than one person to make a date, and the same applies to both this book and the show.

I'd like to begin by thanking Jay Hunt, Nick Mirsky, Madonna Benjamin, Rita Daniels and everyone at Channel 4 for commissioning *First Dates*; to Ana de Moraes who dreamed it up, Meredith Chambers for making it happen, and both Simon Dickson and Nicola Lloyd for turning it into such a success. For their devotion to the cause, I am forever grateful to Molly Sayers, Sarah Fink and Kirsty Warwood, as well as all the cupids in the production team and the Paternoster Chop House for hosting the *First Dates* restaurant.

In bringing the magic of the show to the page, I'd like to thank Matt Whyman and Jordan Paramor, as well as Emily Robertson and Joel Rickett, Julian Alexander and Ben Clark for their tireless work behind the scenes. Last, but not least, I should like to thank you, as one of the millions of viewers who tune in every week in the hope that love will strike and transform lives.

ANSWERS

1. Muhala (FRANKIE & MUHALA)
2. ANNA & LIAM
3. Louis (LOUIS & AMBER)
4. Sophie (SOPHIE & AARON)
5. Michael (KATHLEEN & MICHAEL)
6. Louisa (LOUISA & WILL)
7. Laura (LAURA & MATT)
8. KEITH & LAUREN
9. PAUL & SAMANTHA
10. Ben (HOLLY & BEN)
11. Stephen (GORDON & STEPHEN)
12. Rebecca (REBECCA & DAVID)
13. Luke (HANNAH & LUKE)
14. Rachel (JOEL & RACHEL)
15. EMILY & ALISTAIR
16. Lachlan (LACHLAN & RACHEL)
17. Grace (GRACE & CHUKS)
18. Alexandra (ALEXANDRA & LOUIS)
19. FRANCESCA & HUGO
20. CLAUDIA & MARCUS
21. GEO & CHARLOTTE
22. Marc (MARC & ELLE)
23. Ricky (JACQUI & RICKY)
24. DEAN & KATE
25. Ben (BEN & CHLOE)
26. Thomas (PATRICK & THOMAS)
27. Alex (GEORGIA & ALEX)
28. AMY & ROBERT
29. Lachlan (LACHLAN & BECCA)
30. Luke (LUKE & SHANNON)
31. Thomas (THOMAS & COLIN)
32. LUCIA & OLLIE

PHOTO CREDITS

DAN JOSEPH
WWW.DANJOSEPHPHOTO.COM

pp. 44, 148

DAVID KING
WWW.DAVEKINGPHOTOGRAPHY.COM

pp. 26, 38, 50, 64, 78, 90, 92, 104, 116, 128, 142,
154, 168, 184, 196, 208, 210, 222, 234, 248

RORY MULVEY
WWW.RORYMULVEY.COM

pp. 32, 162, 170

STEPHEN WELLS
WWW.STEPHEN-WELLS.COM

pp. 20, 52, 58, 72, 84, 98, 110, 122, 130, 136,
178, 190, 202, 216, 228, 230, 244